UNITED STATES

Activity & fun Fact Book

50 States

Learn Each State & Capital
130 Puzzles and Coloring

AGES 6+

Hi and thank you for purchasing this book, I look forward to taking this journey across 50 States of America with you. Please read through the instructions below so you know how to navigate the activities. Answers are provided in the back of the book if you get stuck.

If you'd like a printable version of the map and some top secret bonus goodies please go here: www.rocketstudiobooks.com/50states

WORD SCRAMBLE & FILL IN THE BLANKS

You will find all of the words in the word scramble and fill in the blanks within the two pages on each state. For word scramble you need to put the letters in the correct order to make the words and for fill in the blanks you better make sure you have read all of the fun facts!

WORD SEARCH

Find the words in the word search. They can go left to right, up and down, diagonally and even backwards. We didn't say it would be easy!

WORD MATCH

You will find all of the words within the two pages on each state. Draw a line to match the words together.

CROSSWORD

You will find all of the answers within the two pages on each state. Some of the answers may contain two or more words. There are no spaces in the crossword, so just make two words into one, i.e. Lake Tahoe is LAKETAHOE.

CRACK THE CODE

You have to decipher the code by finding the letter in the key that matches the number.

DOT TO DOT

Start at the number 1 and connect the dots. When you get to the end make sure you go back to one, then you can color in!

BEFORE YOU START

You need to know your north from south and east from west.
Check out the compass if you get stuck.

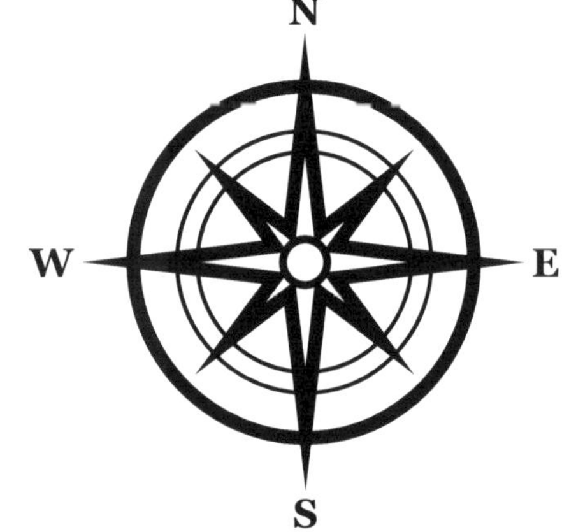

COLOR THE USA!

LABEL & COLOR THE MAP

By the end of this book you'll know all about the 50 States of America.

Come back to this page and write in the name of each state. You might want to save your coloring of this page till last too. Go to the website on the opposite page to get a copy of this map if you want to color straight away, or write down the names on each state as you work your way through the book.

COUNT & COLOR THE BIRDS

As you work your way through the book, you will notice lots of states have the same state birds. Count them as you go and write the total here.

Count the American Robin's: _ _

Count the Western Meadowlark's: _ _

Count the Mockingbird's: _ _

THE ADVENTURES OF BORIS THE BEAR

Boris the bear has escaped from one of Mrs Huntington's books for small children. He was told he doesn't belong in a geography book for big kids, but he is stubborn and sneaky and has made his way onto some of the pages. Can you circle every time you see him and write down the total number of times you see him here _ _

If you enjoy this book it would mean a lot to Mrs Huntington if you could please leave a review where you purchased it.

ALABAMA

Blackberry was declared the state fruit in 2004, at the request of Fairhope Elementary School. What would you declare a state fruit?

CAPITAL CITY: Montgomery
POPULATION: 5,040,000
REGION: Southeast / East South Central
ABBREVIATION: AL
STATE FLOWER: Camellia
STATE TREE: Longleaf Pine
STATE BIRD: Yellowhammer
STATE NICKNAME: The Yellowhammer State
NATURAL WONDER: Wetumpka Crater

DIXIE or Dixieland is a nickname for the Southern United States.

WORD SCRAMBLE

CTEKOR	_ _ _ _ _ _
TFALOOLB	_ _ _ _ _ _ _ _
RONI	_ _ _ _
ELETS	_ _ _ _ _
TTNOCO	_ _ _ _ _ _
ASAN	_ _ _ _
LIIVC	_ _ _ _ _
EALCRBBYKR	_ _ _ _ _ _ _ _ _ _
EDIIX	_ _ _ _ _

Alabama is home to NASA and the largest spaceflight museum in the world, housing rockets and artifacts from space exploration.

It is the only state in America to have all major natural resources to make iron and steel.

Also known for its college football culture, Alabama was the "Cotton Kingdom" in the 1800s and central to the Civil War.

DRAW ON THE MAP
FLORENCE
HUNTSVILLE
BIRMINGHAM
TUSCALOOSA
AUBURN
SELMA
MONTGOMERY
MOBILE
PEANUT
Grace's High Falls
North East of Birmingham, close to the Georgia border.
Edmund Pettus Bridge
South of Selma, across the Alabama River.
NASA
North of Birmingham
Peanut Butter Festival
Brundidge
Southeast of Montgomery

ALASKA

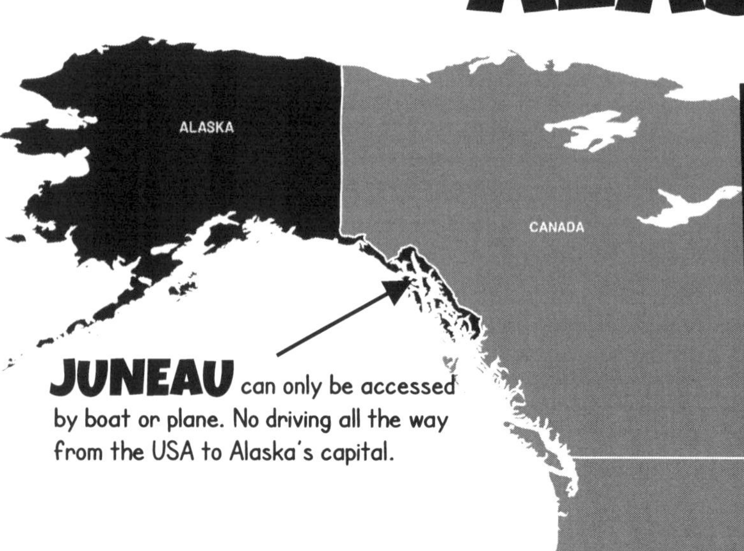

JUNEAU can only be accessed by boat or plane. No driving all the way from the USA to Alaska's capital.

CAPITAL CITY: Juneau
POPULATION: 732,673
REGION: Extreme Pacific Northwest
ABBREVIATION: AK
STATE FLOWER: Alpine Forget-Me-Not
STATE TREE: Sitka Spruce
STATE BIRD: Willow Ptarmigan(Grouse)
STATE NICKNAME: The Last Frontier
NATURAL WONDER: Northern Lights

Alaska is the largest state in the United States, covering 663,267 square miles.

DIRECTIONS

Follow the directions to write the names of the cities in the labels.

JUNEAU: The top label in the Southeast corner of Alaska

ANCHORAGE: Under the lighthouse

FAIRBANKS: Under Boris the bear; Northeast from Anchorage

KETCHIKAN: The most Southeastern point

SITKA: West of Juneau and Ketchikan

WORD SEARCH

C	N	B	E	A	D	W	V	S	T	C	P	N	W	V
P	O	E	Z	R	I	F	F	S	H	T	G	R	N	Q
Y	J	P	N	T	U	N	D	R	A	Q	V	U	I	J
M	S	W	W	G	C	T	G	L	A	C	I	E	R	S
O	M	L	H	G	R	A	N	N	E	N	V	J	F	Q
X	I	L	E	M	U	U	O	E	Q	L	C	C	T	F
H	G	P	U	R	D	M	V	F	V	O	G	G	Z	E
D	O	D	O	K	L	F	C	X	A	D	C	D	G	H
V	L	R	V	A	A	I	N	S	B	R	A	A	X	Y
A	A	A	S	M	S	N	T	O	P	E	R	F	Y	E
P	Q	U	T	C	U	L	W	B	V	O	A	L	O	X
M	W	Q	V	F	I	C	E	B	H	M	R	R	F	P
E	S	O	Q	N	Q	P	M	C	N	M	W	Y	S	H
K	Q	P	E	C	G	N	N	N	D	Y	C	R	R	F
K	V	Z	L	W	E	A	M	F	J	U	N	E	A	U

ADVENTURE
ANCHORAGE
AURORA

BEARS
COASTLINE
GLACIERS

JUNEAU
SALMON
TUNDRA

The largest national forest in America, the Tongass National Forest covers most of Southeast Alaska. This state also has more coastline than all other U.S. states combined!

Alaska is home to polar bears, beluga whales and walruses. It also has the world's largest brown bear, the Kodiak. ROAR!

ARIZONA

CAPITAL CITY: Phoenix
POPULATION: 7,276,000
REGION: Southwest / Mountain States
ABBREVIATION: AZ
STATE FLOWER: Saguaro Cactus
STATE TREE: Palo Verde
STATE BIRD: Cactus Wren
STATE NICKNAME: Grand Canyon State
NATURAL WONDER: Grand Canyon

PHOENIX
is the fifth largest city by population in the USA.

Arizona is only the state in the contiguous US that touches four corners (in the Northeast), known as the Four Corners Monument. Home to the Grand Canyon, the London Bridge (from England!) and Barringer Meteorite Crater, also known as Meteor Crater, nearly 1 mile wide.

Jerome is the largest Ghost Town in America, once a booming copper mining town, but since abandoned.

WORD MATCHES

FOUR	TOWN
SAGUARO	BRIDGE
GHOST	DATE
METEOR	CACTUS
COPPER	BREAD
LONDON	CORNERS
FRY	CRATER
MEDJOOL	MINING

The food in Arizona is heavily influenced by Mexico. You must try fry bread, chimichanga and medjool dates, although not all at once.

Can you make your way from the north of Arizona to the south?

If you like the sun, then Arizona is your state. Yuma, in the South Western corner of the state, holds the record for the most recorded hours of sunshine in a year, averaging 4,000 hours annually.

Color in this photo and then label the natural wonder.

ARKANSAS

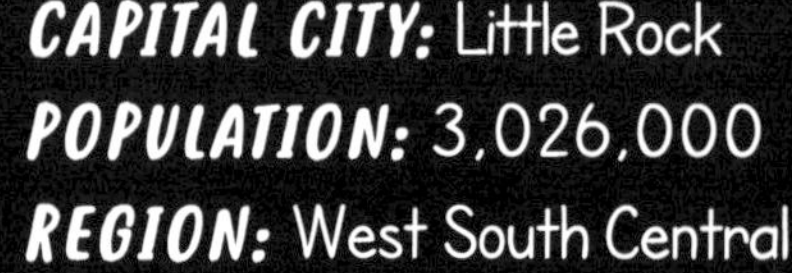

CAPITAL CITY: Little Rock
POPULATION: 3,026,000
REGION: West South Central
ABBREVIATION: AR
STATE FLOWER: Apple Blossom
STATE TREE: Pine
STATE BIRD: Mockingbird
STATE NICKNAME: The Natural State
NATURAL WONDER: Blanchard Springs Caverns

LITTLE ROCK is named after a small rock formation on the south bank of the Arkansas River, this rock served as a landmark for early explorers and traders.

MISSING LETTERS

1. Li_ _le R_c_
2. Pi_ _ _om_ _o
3. _ock_ng_i_d
4. Ap_ _e Bl_ _s_m
5. R_ _e
6. Nat_ _a_ S_a_e
7. C_v_ _n_
8. M_ _n_ai_
9. _i_e_
10. Fo_e_t

Arkansas is called the Natural State because of its abundance of natural beauty including mountains, rivers, caves and forests.

The national fruit *and* vegetable is the pink tomato (although it doesn't look that pink, more a shade just before red). Go on, color in that tomato pink!

Speaking of food, Arkansas is the largest producer of rice in America, this is mostly in the eastern part of the state.

COLOR IN THE CAVERNS

Color in the caverns below. If you don't know what colors to do, ask your parent if you can search together for Blanchard Springs Caverns. You'll see a lot of brown rocks and sandy colors.

CALIFORNIA

CAPITAL CITY: Sacramento
POPULATION: 39,029,342
REGION: West / Pacific Coast
ABBREVIATION: CA
STATE FLOWER: California Poppy
STATE TREE: California Redwood
STATE BIRD: Valley Quail (California Quail)
STATE NICKNAME: The Golden State
NATURAL WONDER: Yosemite's Firefall

SACRAMENTO became the capital because it is in the middle of the state.

WORD SEARCH

BEACHES
GRAPES
HOLLYWOOD
NAPA
PALMS
SUNSHINE
SURFING
TACOS
YOSEMITE

```
L H C A Y H N R I E S K F I V
U A O A R E L E G Q Y S Z B M
R H A L H Y O S E M I T E E V
N O X L L G N Y V P I P T A C
X E O M H Y R L H H A P X C N
U J K Z S S W A F B Y L R H A
S T N E T O Q O P G X Q M E P
U M G N C S L U O E R N G S A
R L R A R K S Z R D S I C U M
F I N I F M Q Z X O T P Z N J
I J V D O Q M P J A D C L S Z
N L A Y P V B X C M W T Q H N
G S H X H N I O G L E W M I W
U I A Q D M S G B Q C V M N I
Q L T U O O N K Y X Y M N E J
```

California has the most number of people living in its state. And it's not just because of Hollywood, its large coastal regions, mild weather and economy make it pretty attractive.

DRAW ON THE MAP

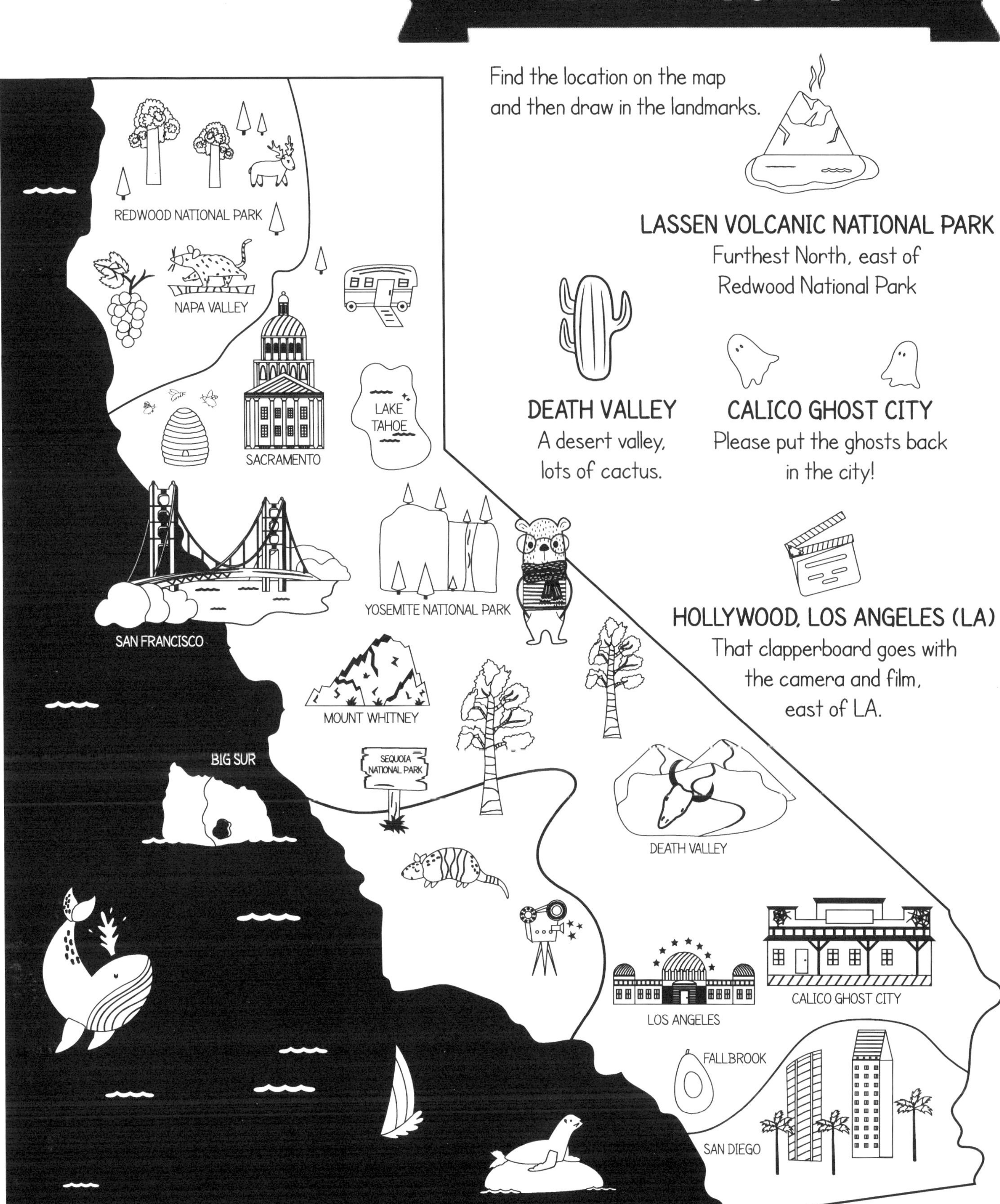

COLORADO

DENVER is one the highest major cities in the USA, sitting at one mile above sea level.

CAPITAL CITY: Denver
POPULATION: 5,812,000
REGION: West / Mountain States
ABBREVIATION: CO
STATE FLOWER: Colorado Columbine
STATE TREE: Blue Spruce
STATE BIRD: Lark Bunting
STATE NICKNAME: The Centennial State
NATURAL WONDER: Rocky Mountain National Park

Colorado got its name from Spanish explorers who saw the river running through the state had a muddy, red color to it. Colorado is actually broken into "colored red".

Colorado is well known for skiing around the Rocky Mountains. Locations such as Aspen, Vail and Telluride are in the region.

In addition to skiing, the state is well known for its outdoor lifestyle, hiking and camping in nature among wildlife, rivers and wildflowers.

WORD SCRAMBLE

GNIISK _ _ _ _ _ _
DRE _ _ _
SNIHPSA _ _ _ _ _ _ _
OEDWRLIFLWS _ _ _ _ _ _ _ _ _ _ _
OAROOLDC _ _ _ _ _ _ _ _
NUITNOASM _ _ _ _ _ _ _ _ _
RUNATE _ _ _ _ _ _
SEIRRV _ _ _ _ _ _
PNGMICA _ _ _ _ _ _ _

STATE MAZE

Can you make your way from the northwest of Colorado to the southeast?

SOLVE THE SEQUENCE

Draw the item that comes next in the sequence:

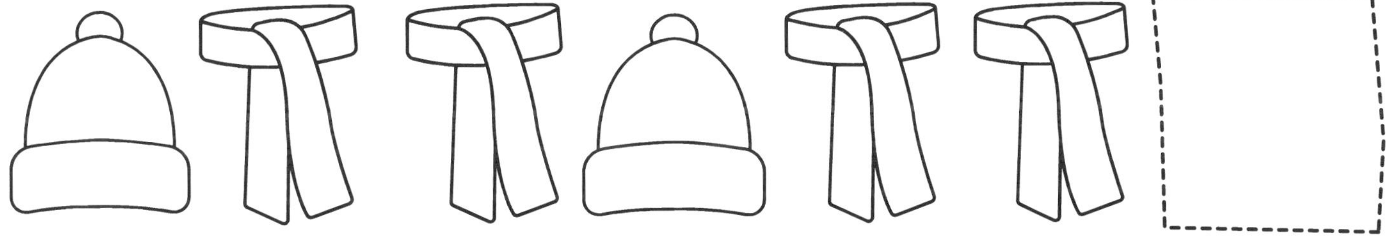

CONNECTICUT

CAPITAL CITY: Hartford
POPULATION: 3,606,000
REGION: Northeast / New England
ABBREVIATION: CT
STATE FLOWER: Mountain Laurel
STATE TREE: Charter Oak
STATE BIRD: American Robin
STATE NICKNAME: Constitution State
NATURAL WONDER: Dinosaur State Park

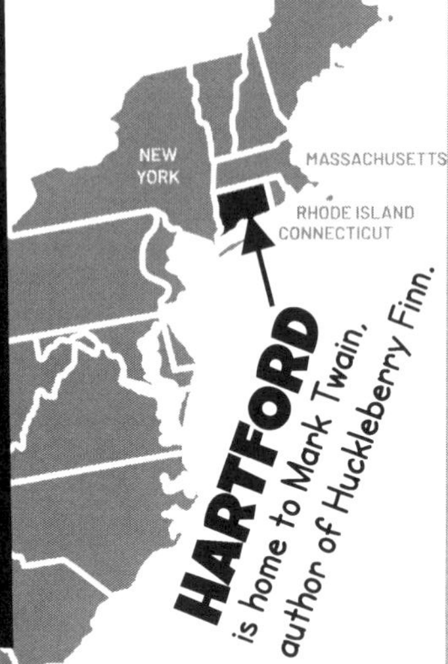

There was once a time in Connecticut when something quite nutty was happening. In the late 19th Century, peddlers would sometimes trick customers into buying wood instead of nutmeg. So Connecticut is also known as "The Nutmeg State".

Dinosaur tracks were discovered in Rocky Hill in 1966 and now you can walk in dino footprints at the Dinosaur State Park.

Connecticut is known for its coastal beauty, especially along Long Island Sound and historic small towns.

WORD MATCHES

MOUNTAIN	ISLAND
AMERICAN	FINN
NEW	ENGLAND
MARK	BEAUTY
CHARTER	HILL
ROCKY	STATE
COASTAL	OAK
LONG	ROBIN
HUCKLEBERRY	TWAIN
NUTMEG	LAUREL

DOT TO DOT

The first constitution ever written in the United States was in Connecticut in 1639. These were rules and laws which applied to the state and they gave voters the right to elect government.

"Connecticut" comes from a native American word which means "beside the long tidal river", which is a reference to the Connecticut River.

DELAWARE

CAPITAL CITY: Dover
POPULATION: 1,003,000
REGION: Northeast / Mid Atlantic
ABBREVIATION: DE
STATE FLOWER: Peach Blossom
STATE TREE: American Holly
STATE BIRD: Blue Hen Chicken
STATE NICKNAME: The First State
NATURAL WONDER: Blanchard Springs Caverns

PENNSYLVANIA
NEW JERSEY
DELAWARE
MARYLAND

DOVER is named after Dover in Kent, England. In fact all counties in Delaware are British names.

Color that chicken blue!

MISSING LETTERS

1. B_u_ _en
2. M_ _ A_l_ _ti_
3. _ _rs_ S_a_e
4. _e_ Ca_ _le
5. Bl_ _ _b_r_
6. S_am_ _an_
7. _en_
8. Pea_ _ _ _os_o_
9. _ _s_e_
10. Re_ _e_

Delaware is called the First State because it become the first of the 13 original states to join the United States in 1787.

Delaware is the second smallest state after Rhode Island. It is mostly covered by the low Atlantic Coastal Plain with three state forests: Blackbird, Taber and Redden. At the southern border the plain is swampland.

There are only three counties in Delaware: New Castle, Kent and Sussex.

Delaware has more chickens than people. There are roughly two million chickens in the state and one million people!

COLORIFIC CHICKENS

OK so you have a blue chicken on the other page, how about making these ones rainbow chickens?

CRACK THE CODE*

Discover the area that mostly covers Delaware

__ __ __ __ __ __ __ __
11 18 10 11 7 18 22 25

__ __ __ __ __ __ __
25 4 11 1 18 11 10

__ __ __ __ __
2 10 11 22 7

KEY

1	2	3	4	5	6	7	8	9	10	11	12	13	14	15	16	17	18	19	20	21	22	23	24	25
S	P	V	O	Z	D	N	H	G	L	A	E	J	X	U	W	M	T	B	Q	R	I	F	K	C

*Not the egg...bad puns included!

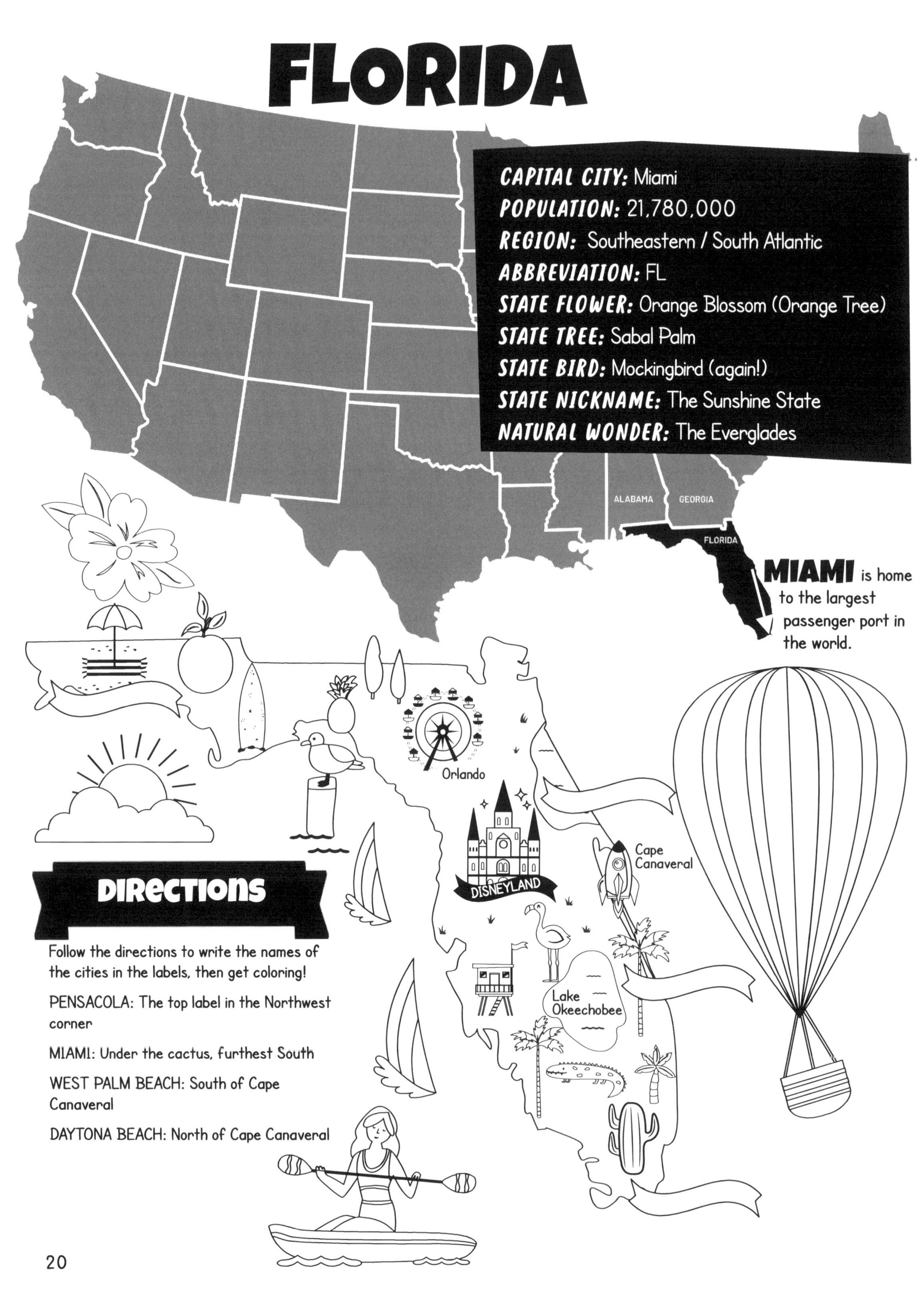
FLORIDA
CAPITAL CITY: Miami
POPULATION: 21,780,000
REGION: Southeastern / South Atlantic
ABBREVIATION: FL
STATE FLOWER: Orange Blossom (Orange Tree)
STATE TREE: Sabal Palm
STATE BIRD: Mockingbird (again!)
STATE NICKNAME: The Sunshine State
NATURAL WONDER: The Everglades
ALABAMA
GEORGIA
FLORIDA
MIAMI is home to the largest passenger port in the world.
Orlando
DISNEYLAND
Cape Canaveral
Lake Okeechobee
DIRECTIONS
Follow the directions to write the names of the cities in the labels, then get coloring!
PENSACOLA: The top label in the Northwest corner
MIAMI: Under the cactus, furthest South
WEST PALM BEACH: South of Cape Canaveral
DAYTONA BEACH: North of Cape Canaveral

WORD SEARCH

P	W	S	L	E	R	R	U	S	D	B	S	E	D	X
Y	M	R	J	I	M	A	I	M	L	Y	N	U	K	N
Z	G	Y	E	Y	R	C	G	E	X	I	V	U	G	A
R	H	U	Z	T	D	C	H	A	H	O	K	F	Z	L
F	M	P	B	H	I	J	O	S	F	E	B	E	N	L
H	G	I	L	G	Y	R	N	S	Y	Y	B	F	E	I
U	Y	G	A	P	Y	U	E	S	S	W	C	V	E	G
U	K	R	J	M	S	C	B	M	O	P	E	D	Q	A
J	M	R	E	D	I	E	Z	O	E	R	R	G	H	T
L	Z	D	X	A	A	O	R	B	G	N	P	H	G	O
U	X	G	O	C	Y	A	Y	L	L	M	T	J	E	R
N	P	O	H	Q	N	U	A	C	X	J	U	C	M	S
E	C	E	L	G	A	D	I	W	Q	O	A	J	S	W
D	S	E	E	R	E	B	H	I	Z	P	I	C	U	C
W	T	S	S	S	D	U	M	S	S	U	U	Y	L	I

ALLIGATORS
BEACHES
EVERGLADES

KEYS
MIAMI
ORANGES

RETIREMENT
SPACE
SUNSHINE

Florida has a chain of about 1700 islands off the southern coast called the Florida Keys, only around 30 islands have people living on them.

Before you reach the Keys, you'll find the Everglades, a vast tropical wetland. 1.5 million acres of mangroves & marshes home to hundreds of animal species.

GEORGIA

CAPITAL CITY: Atlanta
POPULATION: 10,800,000
REGION: Southeastern / South Atlantic
ABBREVIATION: GA
STATE FLOWER: Cherokee Rose
STATE BIRD: Brown Thrasher
STATE TREE: Live Oak
STATE NICKNAME: The Peach State
NATURAL WONDER: Radium Springs

ATLANTA is the unofficial capital of the South. It has the busiest airport in the world!

DRAW A PEACH

1.
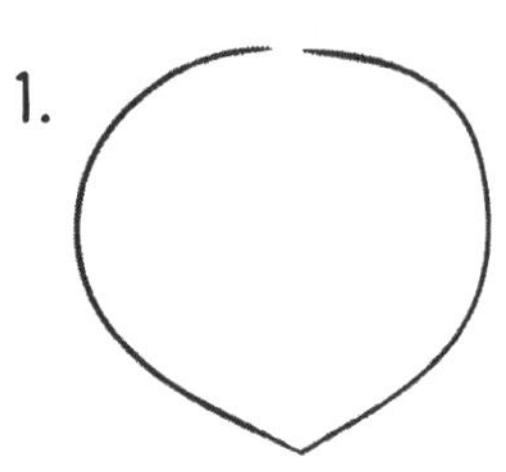

2.
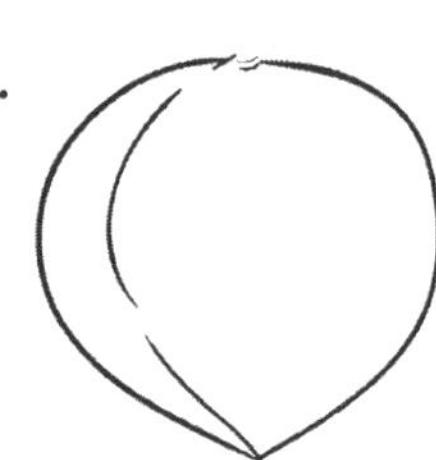

3.

4.

5.

6. *Your turn*

Radium Springs in Albany, GA has waters that are consistently 68 degrees, so there is no running out of hot water there! They also contain traces of radium (Ra), hence the name.

Georgia has 15 barrier islands (a sandbar that has become an island) including Tybee Island and Jekyll Island.

Stone Mountain is a massive ancient, quartz dome shaped rock near Atlanta.

Georgia is also the birthplace of Martin Luther King Jr.

CROSSWORD

Across

2 Tybee & Jekyll are these
6 His first names are Martin Luther
7 A giant rock in Georgia
9 Unofficial capital of the South

Down

1 Summertime, fuzzy fruit
3 Hot water that comes out of the ground
4 Largest swamp in North America
5 Indians native to Georgia's coast
8 Symbol for Radium
10 State tree

The Yamacraw Indians lived in coastal Georgia in the 1700s.

Georgia also has the largest swamp in North America, the Okefenokee Swamp, covering 700 square miles.

HAWAII

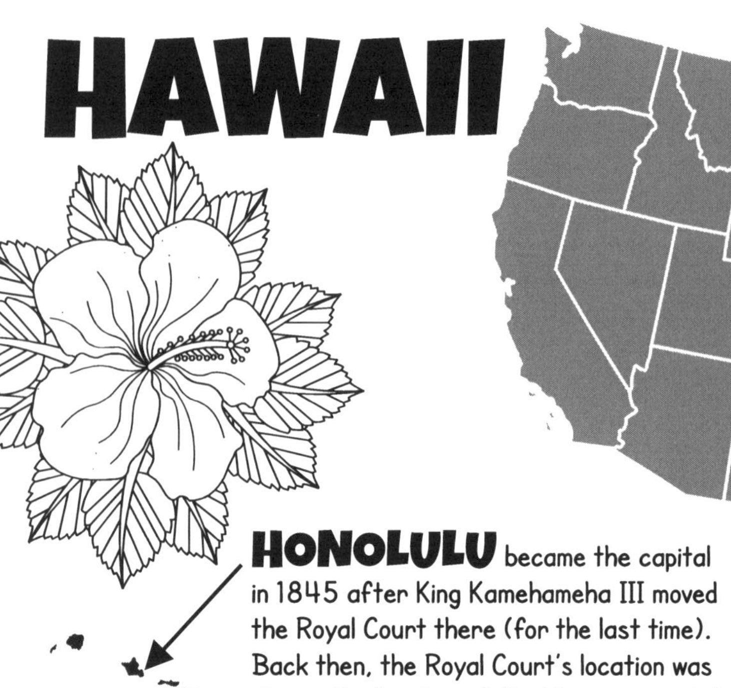

CAPITAL CITY: Honolulu
POPULATION: 1,442,000
REGION: Pacific
ABBREVIATION: HI
STATE FLOWER: Yellow Hibiscus
STATE TREE: Kukui, Candlenut
STATE BIRD: Nene
STATE NICKNAME: The Aloha State
NATURAL WONDER: Volcanoes National Park

HONOLULU became the capital in 1845 after King Kamehameha III moved the Royal Court there (for the last time). Back then, the Royal Court's location was always the location of the Hawaiian capital.

HAWAII

There are only a few islands of Hawaii in our illustration, but Hawaii actually has 132 different islands! The main islands are Oahu, Maui, Kauai, Big Island, Molokai, Lanai, Niihau and Kaho'olawe.

NEWSFLASH: Mauna Kea on the Big Island is the tallest mountain in the world! If you thought Mount Everest is the tallest mountain, you are still correct, unless you measure from below the sea, in which case Mauna Kea is the winner.

Hawaii is the only state in North America that grows coffee. That tropical climate and volcanic soil makes Hawaii suitable for growing all kinds of crops.

WORD SCRAMBLE

EOCEFF _ _ _ _ _ _
UHCBISSI _ _ _ _ _ _ _ _
OALAH _ _ _ _ _
ASEVLONOC _ _ _ _ _ _ _ _ _
OHLOUNLU _ _ _ _ _ _ _ _
UIAM _ _ _ _
DSLIAN _ _ _ _ _ _
UOAMTNIN _ _ _ _ _ _ _ _
ACPILOTR _ _ _ _ _ _ _ _
ELTICAM _ _ _ _ _ _ _

DIRECTIONS

Follow the directions to write the names of the islands:

NIHAU: Furthest Northwest

HAWAII: Furthest Southeast

MOLOKAI: Southeast of Oahu

MAUI: Northwest neighbor to Hawaii

LANAI: Small island south of Molokai

KAUAI: Northwest neighbor to Oahu

IDAHO

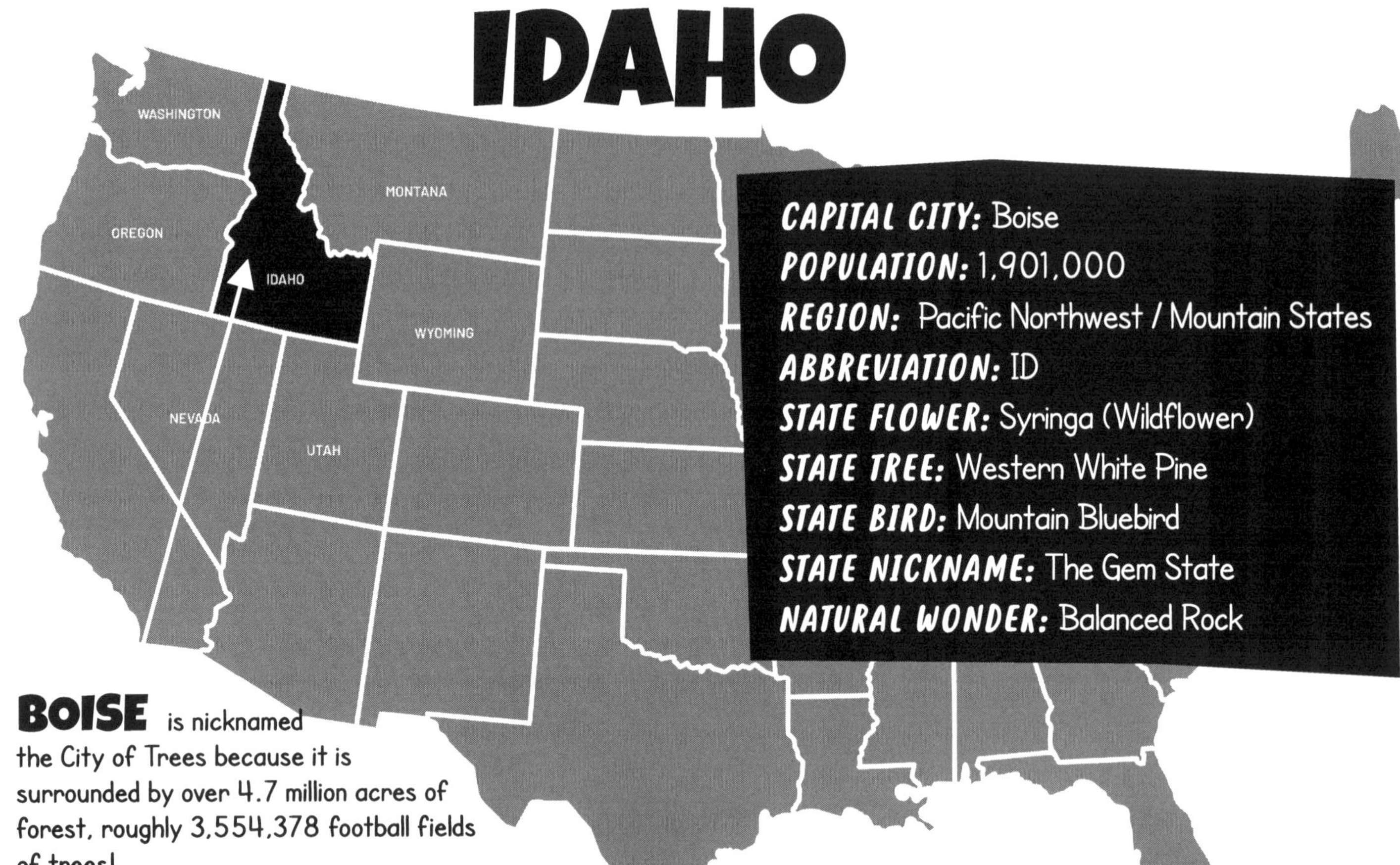

CAPITAL CITY: Boise
POPULATION: 1,901,000
REGION: Pacific Northwest / Mountain States
ABBREVIATION: ID
STATE FLOWER: Syringa (Wildflower)
STATE TREE: Western White Pine
STATE BIRD: Mountain Bluebird
STATE NICKNAME: The Gem State
NATURAL WONDER: Balanced Rock

BOISE is nicknamed the City of Trees because it is surrounded by over 4.7 million acres of forest, roughly 3,554,378 football fields of trees!

WORD MATCHES

MOUNTAIN	RESOURCES
BALANCED	GARNET
GEM	BLUEBIRD
SHOSHONE	PINE
NATURAL	ROCK
ROCKY	STATE
BLACK	FALLS
BIGHORN	BEARS
WHITE	SHEEP
STAR	MOUNTAINS

Shoshone Falls, in Twin Falls is one of the largest natural waterfalls in the United States, it's bigger than Niagara Falls.

Idaho has an abundance of gems like star garnets, amethysts, rubies and diamonds, earning its rightful nickname, The Gem State.

The Rocky Mountains pass right through Idaho and into Canada, who shares a border with Idaho. Within the Rockies live black bears, grizzly bears, moose bighorn sheep and mountain goats.

CRACK THE CODE

Unearth the gems in Idaho

__ __ __ __ __ __ __ __
24 8 19 15 1 13 17 15

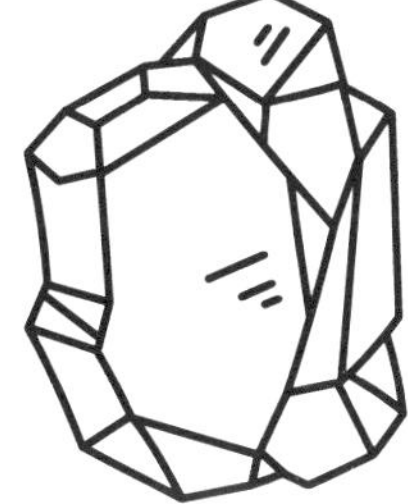

__ __ __ __
20 23 22 13

__ __ __ __ __ __ __
16 25 24 8 6 5 16

__ __ __ __   __ __ __ __ __ __
17 15 24 20   3 24 20 5 19 15

KEY

1	2	3	4	5	6	7	8	9	10	11	12	13	14	15	16	17	18	19	20	21	22	23	24	25
H	F	G	K	N	O	P	M	Z	C	X	L	Y	W	T	D	S	V	E	R	Q	B	U	A	I

ILLINOIS

CAPITAL CITY: Springfield
POPULATION: 12,670,000
REGION: Midwest / East North Central
ABBREVIATION: IL
STATE FLOWER: Violet
STATE TREE: White Oak
STATE BIRD: Northern Cardinal
STATE NICKNAME: The Prairie State
NATURAL WONDER: Garden of the Gods

SPRINGFIELD is known as the hometown of Abraham Lincoln.

CITY SEARCH

N	N	Q	B	R	H	B	F	X	R	P	R	R	O	E
P	A	Q	A	R	M	X	B	I	D	G	A	K	L	X
P	G	R	O	C	K	F	O	R	D	P	B	L	N	D
K	E	H	Y	R	V	F	E	E	X	J	I	U	L	M
E	K	S	R	S	O	L	W	C	O	V	N	E	W	S
C	U	H	K	W	G	M	H	L	R	J	I	O	T	N
B	A	W	R	I	D	B	I	E	T	F	B	F	G	Q
F	W	O	N	O	X	E	P	R	G	Q	H	I	J	N
G	Q	I	T	J	T	A	A	N	Y	L	A	T	E	E
Q	N	A	E	E	N	V	I	X	Q	P	H	W	A	I
H	R	I	G	W	D	R	C	X	M	Z	B	G	R	R
E	O	R	S	O	P	J	L	A	Y	B	V	Y	O	I
A	I	O	C	S	T	A	H	E	W	T	T	T	R	O
G	T	E	O	G	A	C	I	H	C	X	U	M	U	F
V	E	P	C	C	Z	I	U	K	S	J	U	D	A	D

AURORA
CHAMPAIGN
CHICAGO
ELGIN
JOLIET
NAPERVILLE
PEORIA
ROCKFORD
SPRINGFIELD
WAUKEGAN

Springfield may be the capital of Illinois, but you are probably more familiar with Chicago, known as "The Windy City".

The Willis Tower (formerly the Sears Tower) in Chicago was the tallest building in America, until 2020. The construction of One World Trade Center and Central Park Tower in New York beat it by 30 meters.

Illinois used to be covered in prairie grass, hence its nickname.

DIRECTIONS

Follow the directions to write in the names of the cities.

CHICAGO: South of the Ferris Wheel (called Centennial Wheel)

ST LOUIS: Under the arch (called the Gateway Arch)*

SPRINGFIELD: West of Route 66

ROCKFORD: Furthest Northwest

PEORIA: Southwest of Rockford

AURORA: Under the Paramount Theater (cinema)

*Technically in Missouri, but just on the border of the Mississippi River.

INDIANA

CAPITAL CITY: Indianapolis
POPULATION: 6,806,000
REGION: Midwestern / East North Central
ABBREVIATION: IN
STATE FLOWER: Peony
STATE BIRD: Cardinal
STATE NICKNAME: The Hoosier State
NATURAL WONDER: Creek State Park

INDIANAPOLIS

Vroooom...Indianapolis is the "Racing Capital of the World" and home to the Indy 500, a 500 mile race famous around the world.

MICHIGAN
ILLINOIS
INDIANA
OHIO
KENTUCKY

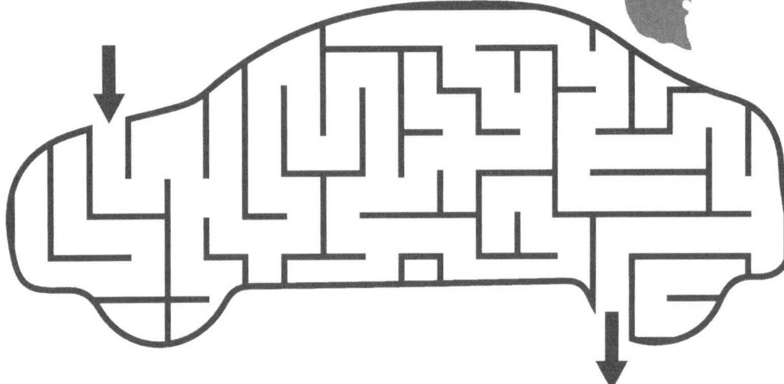

Indiana is named by Europeans in honor of the American Indian tribes who lived in the region when they arrived.

Indiana is home to an archaeological site called Angel Mounds. People lived here between 1000 and 1450, so over 500 years ago.

MISSING LETTERS*

1. I_d_ 5_ _
2. _rc_i_s
3. H_ _si_ _ St_ _e
4. C_ _n Ma_e
5. An_e_ _oun_s
6. P_ _r Ca_ _us
7. _mer_ca_ I_ _ia_
8. Ba_e_a_l
9. _ic_en Mo_ _e_
10. Sa_ _ D_ _es

*and numbers

MAZE

Head from north to south.

Indiana is famous for its corn, and with that comes corn mazes! Many of the corn mazes create designs that are visible from above. For example, in Waterloo they created a Pokemon design to celebrate the 25th anniversary.

The very first professional baseball game took place in Fort Worth, IN in 1871.

Great big sand dunes, called the Indiana dunes are north around Lake Michigan and are home to unusual plants like prickly pear cactus, lichen mosses and bearberry, as well as more than 20 types of orchids.

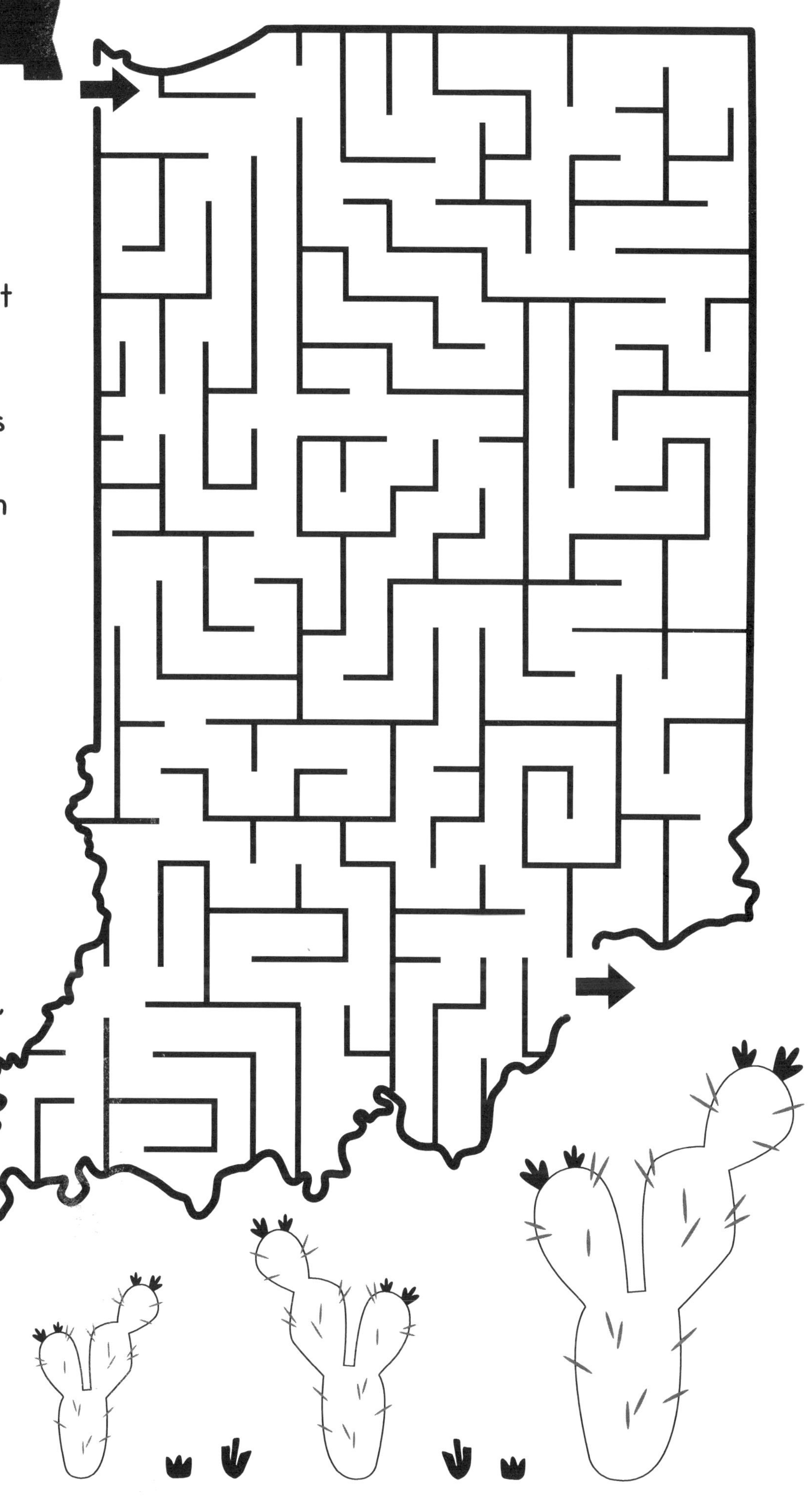

IOWA

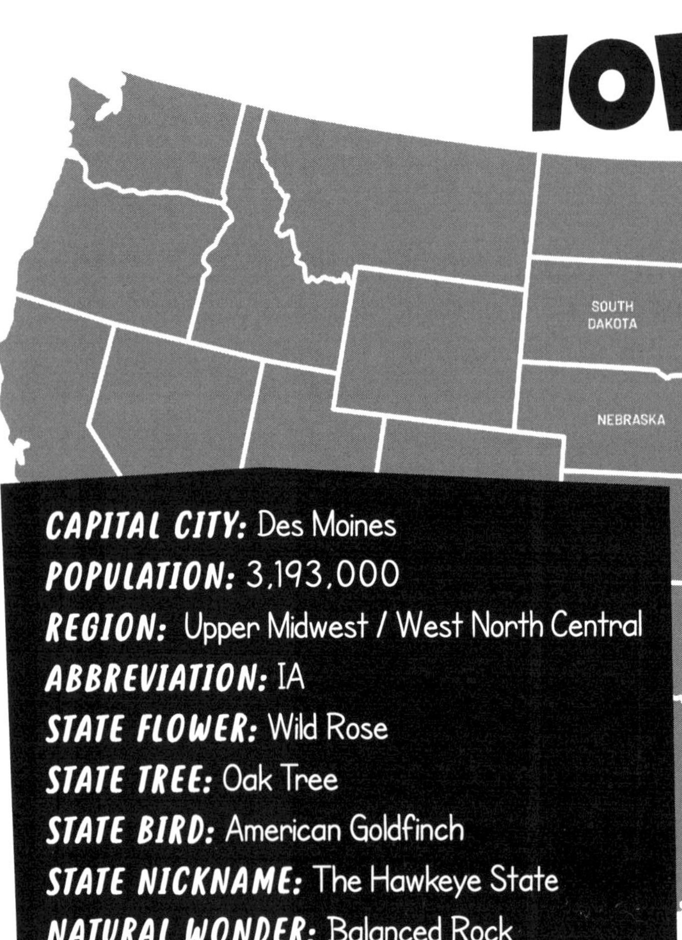

MINNESOTA
WISCONSIN
IOWA
ILLINOIS
MISSOURI

CAPITAL CITY: Des Moines
POPULATION: 3,193,000
REGION: Upper Midwest / West North Central
ABBREVIATION: IA
STATE FLOWER: Wild Rose
STATE TREE: Oak Tree
STATE BIRD: American Goldfinch
STATE NICKNAME: The Hawkeye State
NATURAL WONDER: Balanced Rock

"The Hawkeye State" nickname was inspired by a Native American warrior named Black Hawk (a local Iowan) and/or the character of Hawkeye in *The Last of the Mohicans*.

Common mammals include red foxes, squirrels, weasels and white-tailed deer.

Iowa's greatest natural resource is its rich soil, which grows corn and soybeans. In fact Iowa grows the most corn in the United States.

Iowa's name comes from the Native American Tribe Iowa, also known as the Ioway.

DES MOINES was originally called Fort Raccoon, but it was said to be "not a dignified name for a Fort", so it become a fancy French name, Fort Des Moines and then the Fort was dropped.

DRAW A RED FOX

1.

2.

3.

4.

5.

6. *Your turn*

CROSSWORD

DESIGN A QUARTER

What picture can you draw for the state quarter motto "Foundation in Education"?

Down

2 Common type of deer

3 Iowa grows the most of this crop

4 Capital city

9 State flower

Across

1 The other name for the Iowa Tribe

6 Neighboring state south of Iowa

7 Neighboring state north of Iowa

5 Color of common fox

8 Name of warrior who inspired state nickname

10 State tree

KANSAS

CAPITAL CITY: Topeka
POPULATION: 2,935,000
REGION: Midwest / West North Central
ABBREVIATION: KS
STATE FLOWER: Sunflower
STATE TREE: Cottonwood Tree
STATE BIRD: Western Meadowlark
STATE NICKNAME: The Sunflower State
NATURAL WONDER: Mushroom Rock State Park

TOPEKA is the capital city, but Wichita has a much bigger population.

Kansas has one of the largest areas of tallgrass prairie left in the world. Picture rolling hills with wild green grass, that's what Flint Hills looks like. As well as grass, Kansas also has fields of sunflowers.

The classic story of the Wizard of Oz is set in Kansas. In the story a tornado whisks Dorothy into Oz, it's not far from the truth as Kansas does have a lot of tornadoes!

Kansas is home to an underground salt museum, you can ride through the mine some 650 feet below ground, and see the salt that was formed about 275 million years ago!

A Kansas City museum is home to the world's largest shuttlecocks. There are four scattered across the lawn and they are 18 foot tall!

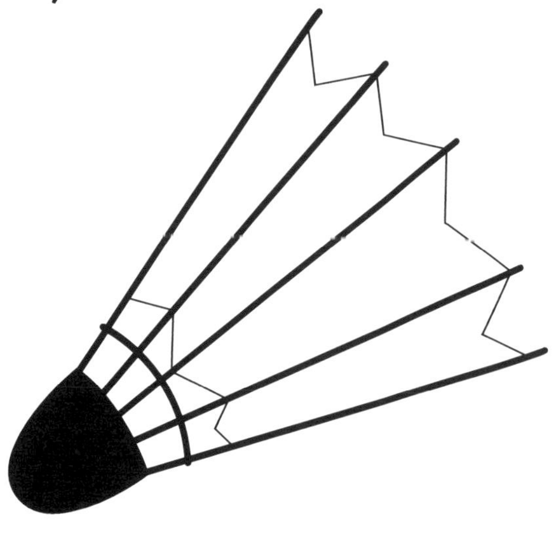

WORD SCRAMBLE

OPAKET _ _ _ _ _ _

EWLFROUSN _ _ _ _ _ _ _ _ _

IMDTSEW _ _ _ _ _ _ _

ATSLLSGRA _ _ _ _ _ _ _ _ _

IIHACTW _ _ _ _ _ _ _

OTANODR _ _ _ _ _ _ _

ZWAIDR _ _ _ _ _ _

ATLS _ _ _ _

NIME _ _ _ _

NODWOOTCOT _ _ _ _ _ _ _ _ _ _

DIRECTIONS

Follow the directions to write the names of the cities on the map below.

KANSAS CITY: Northeast, above the giant shuttlecocks.

COLBY: Northwest above the cowboy boots.

PITTSBURG: South of Kansas City

DODGE CITY: Southwest, between the sunflowers and the cow.

WICHITA: East of Dodge City

SALINA: Southwest of Topeka

KENTUCKY

CAPITAL CITY: Frankfort
POPULATION: 4,509,000
REGION: Southeast / East South Central
ABBREVIATION: KY
STATE FLOWER: Goldenrod
STATE TREE: Tulip Poplar
STATE BIRD: Northern Cardinal
STATE NICKNAME: The Bluegrass State
NATURAL WONDER: Mammoth Cave

FRANKFORT got its name from a crossing called "Frank's Ford" on the Kentucky River in the 1780s.

WORD MATCHES

KENTUCKY	VALLEY
TULIP	COUNTY
NORTHERN	CAVE
BLUEGRASS	DERBY
JEFFERSON	PEARL
ABRAHAM	KNOX
FORT	POPLAR
MAMMOTH	LINCOLN
FRESHWATER	STATE
RIVER	CARDINAL

The Kentucky Derby is a horse race that takes place in Louisville, Kentucky every year since 1875. It is the most watched horse race in the United States.

There are 120 counties in Kentucky, the fourth most of any state. Some you may have heard of: Jefferson County, Madison County and some you may not have: Robertson County (population 2,193).

Abraham Lincoln, 16th President, was born in Hodgenville, Kentucky.

The freshwater pearl is Kentucky's state gemstone and these are found in the Tennessee and Mississippi River Valleys.

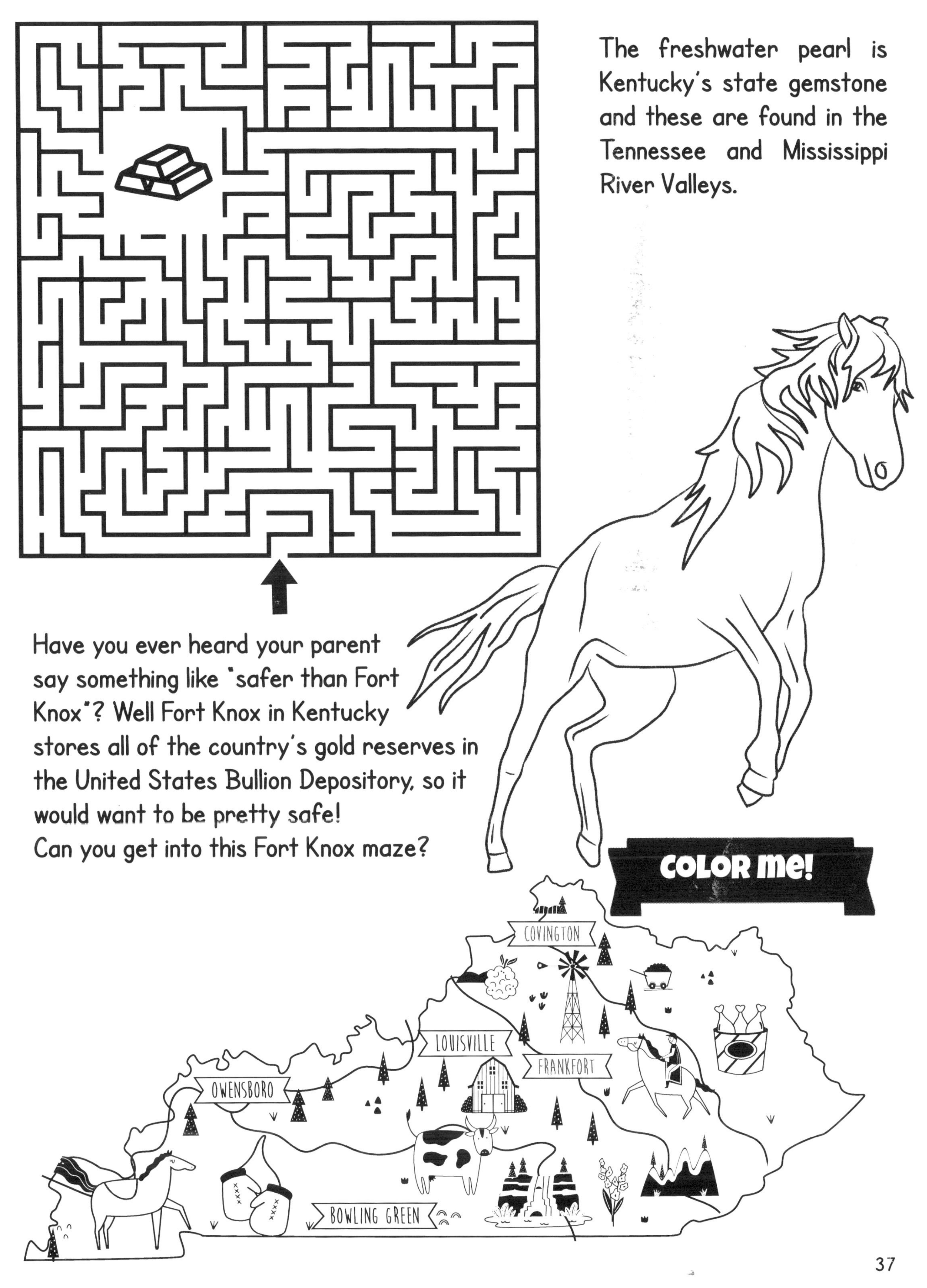

Have you ever heard your parent say something like "safer than Fort Knox"? Well Fort Knox in Kentucky stores all of the country's gold reserves in the United States Bullion Depository, so it would want to be pretty safe!
Can you get into this Fort Knox maze?

LOUISIANA

CAPITAL CITY: Baton Rouge
POPULATION: 4,624,000
REGION: West South Central
ABBREVIATION: LA
STATE FLOWER: Magnolia
STATE TREE: Bald Cypress
STATE BIRD: Brown Pelican
STATE NICKNAME: The Pelican State
NATURAL WONDER: Seven Sisters Oak Tree

BATON ROUGE
means "Red Stick" in French and it is named after a red cypress post that marked a boundary between Native American Tribes.

The Seven Sisters Oak, Madeville, LA is estimated to be 1,500 years old!

Louisiana is known for its Cajun and Creole cultures, this means food and music influenced by French, African and Caribbean heritage.

The Mississippi River runs through Louisiana and is one of the longest rivers in the United States.

New Orleans, Louisiana is often considered the birthplace of jazz music. It was a melting pot of sounds inspired by Caribbean music from the West Indies, beats from Africa and church melodies from the USA.

MISSING LETTERS

1. _at_n R_u_e
2. _re_l_
3. P_l_c_ _ S_a_e
4. S_v_n _is_er_
5. C_ _un
6. B_o_n P_ _ic_n
7. M_s_i_ _i_ _i _i_e_
8. _ew _r_ea_ _
9. J_ _z
10. Ba_d C_pre_ _

DOT TO DOT

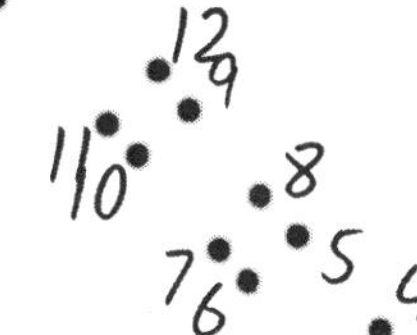

1 2 3 4 5 6 7 8 9 10 11 12 13 14 15 16 17 18 19 20 21 22 23 24 25 26 27 28 29 30 31 32 33 34 35 36 37 38 39 40

COLOR ME IN!

MAINE

AUGUSTA is the easternmost state capital in the United States.

CAPITAL CITY: Augusta
POPULATION: 1,372,000
REGION: Northeastern / New England
ABBREVIATION: ME
STATE FLOWER: White Pine Cone
STATE TREE: Eastern White Pine
STATE BIRD: Chickadee
STATE NICKNAME: The Pine Tree State
NATURAL WONDER: Bay of Fundy

From Ridpath's Universal History, Vol. V, by John Clark Ridpath, 1896

Maine is famous for lobster, supplying nearly 90% of the lobster in the USA.

With all of that coastland comes 4,600 offshore islands, although only 1,200 are more than an acre in size.

Maine is also the only state in the United States with one syllable.

A Norse Viking explorer, Leif Erikson, is said to have sailed to Maine in the year 1000. Native Americans were probably already living on the land then with tribes such as Maliseet, Passamaquoddy, Abenaki and Penobscot notable in Maine.

EYE SPY

Anchor
Mast
Teeth
Viking with 2 hands up
Viking helmet with angel wings

These ones you might have to lookup:
Bow
Crow's nest

WORD SEARCH

G	O	M	T	C	H	V	Z	R	V	F	G	L	D	N
F	E	A	W	P	C	Q	Y	T	D	Z	L	P	M	J
E	S	L	L	B	E	C	W	Z	D	N	C	P	A	Q
E	N	B	L	U	E	B	E	R	R	I	E	S	H	L
S	D	C	I	P	S	O	B	P	B	P	A	Q	Z	Z
O	Y	O	G	K	E	D	W	K	X	M	Y	M	Y	T
O	E	A	E	I	S	S	V	O	Z	A	G	C	F	Z
M	A	S	B	R	U	C	H	I	C	K	A	D	E	E
A	Q	T	S	K	O	K	C	X	O	Q	O	F	A	P
U	K	L	Q	R	H	G	F	E	R	K	Q	I	I	W
G	A	I	L	Q	T	Q	N	P	I	N	E	G	G	S
U	S	N	X	X	H	R	I	A	L	M	I	K	O	E
S	T	E	M	F	G	W	V	R	B	G	Z	K	E	S
T	F	B	C	R	I	X	L	O	B	S	T	E	R	H
A	I	C	Y	F	L	X	J	W	I	W	I	T	H	Q

AUGUSTA
BANGOR
BLUEBERRIES
CHICKADEE
COASTLINE

LIGHTHOUSES
LOBSTER
MOOSE
PINE

MARYLAND

CAPITAL CITY: Annapolis
POPULATION: 6,165,000
REGION: Northeast / Mid Atlantic
ABBREVIATION: MD
STATE FLOWER: Black-Eyed Susan
STATE TREE: White Oak
STATE BIRD: Baltimore Oriole
STATE NICKNAME: The Old Line State & The Free State
NATURAL WONDER: Crystal Grottoes Caverns

ANNAPOLIS is often referred to as the "Sailing Capital of the US." In the 17th century it was also the capital of the USA!

Maryland is one of three states to have an official state cat, and it was the first state to choose a cat. It is the Calico Cat, with the black and gold colors matching the state's official colors.

Whilst Annapolis is the state capital, there are many more populated cities like Baltimore, Columbia and Germantown.

With such a large coastal region, it's no wonder Maryland produces more blue crabs and soft clams than any other state.

Did you know Maryland has its own native animals like the Eastern Mountain Lion and the Gray Wolf?

DOT TO DOT

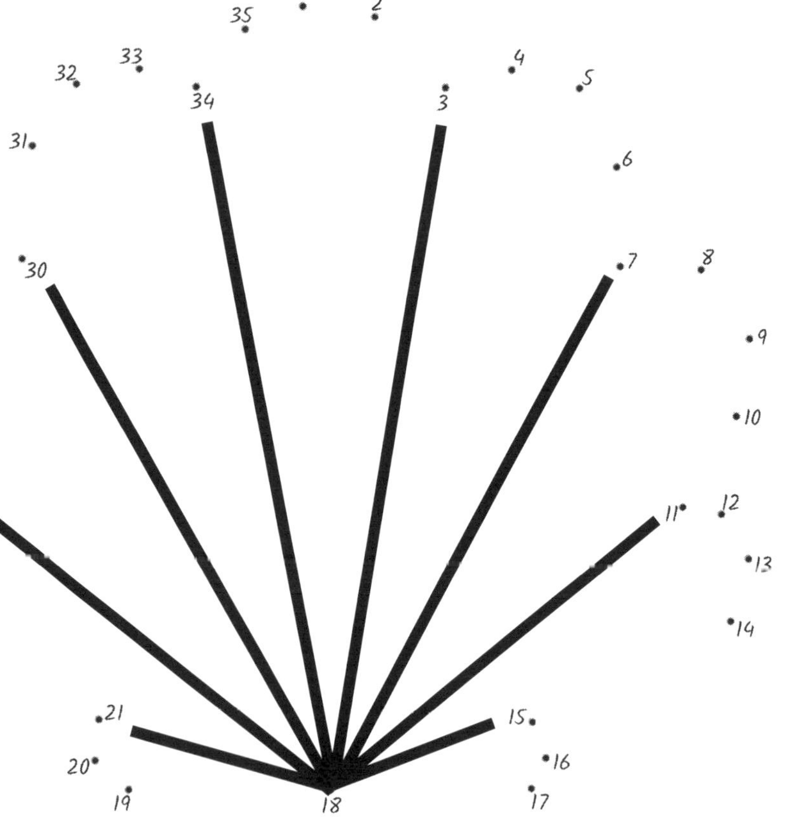

CROSSWORD

Across

1 State nickname

3 Most populated city

5 Type of native wolf

8 State bird

10 The state cat

Down

2 Type of native lion

4 Capital city

6 State tree

7 Produces a lot of this shellfish

9 One of the official state colors

MASSACHUSETTS

BOSTON

is host to one of the oldest and most prestigious marathons in the world, The Boston Marathon.

VERMONT
NEW HAMPSHIRE
MASSACHUSETTS
NEW YORK
RHODE ISLAND
CONNECTICUT

CAPITAL CITY: Boston
POPULATION: 6,985,000
REGION: Northeastern / New England
ABBREVIATION: MA
STATE FLOWER: Mayflower
STATE TREE: American Elm
STATE BIRD: Black-Capped Chickadee
STATE NICKNAME: The Bay State
NATURAL WONDER: Aquinnah Cliffs, Martha's Vineyard

WORD SCRAMBLE

YFMRLWAOE _ _ _ _ _ _ _ _ _ _

DCAKHIECE _ _ _ _ _ _ _ _ _ _

SNBOOT _ _ _ _ _ _ _

IIHGNTGASKNV _ _ _ _ _ _ _ _ _ _ _ _ _ _

MULPOYTH _ _ _ _ _ _ _ _ _

RTA _ _ _

RBAENYRRC _ _ _ _ _ _ _ _ _ _

IEGLHUTOHS _ _ _ _ _ _ _ _ _ _ _ _

LIMPIRG _ _ _ _ _ _ _ _

Massachusetts got its name from a native American tribe called Massachuset.

The first Thanksgiving celebration happened in this state in the town of Plymouth. Maybe that's why the state fruit is a cranberry?!

Also first is the Boston Light built in 1716, the first lighthouse in America. And let's not forget the Mayflower landed in Cape Cod in 1620 with the first English pilgrims.

Ever had a drawing or painting not quite turn out right? You might be able to exhibit at the Museum of Bad Art (MOBA) in Boston. It's a museum dedicated to collecting and displaying the worst art. MOBA aren't being mean, they are celebrating failures, which happen to all of us.

Can you draw a picture suitable for the Museum of Bad Art - maybe one of the Mayflower landing in Cape Cod?

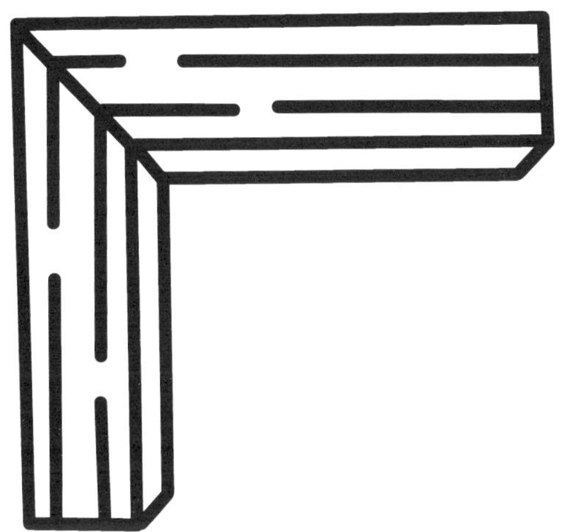
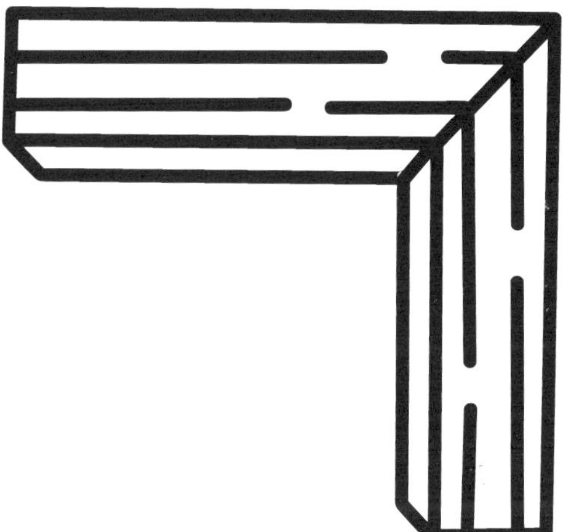

MICHIGAN

CAPITAL CITY: Lansing
POPULATION: 10,050,000
REGION: Upper Midwestern / East North Central
ABBREVIATION: MI
STATE FLOWER: Apple Blossom
STATE TREE: Eastern White Pine
STATE BIRD: American Robin
STATE NICKNAME: The Wolverine State/The Great Lakes
NATURAL WONDER: Eben Ice Caves

Henry Ford built the first car in Detroit and the city is still called "Motor City" because so many cars were made there.

LANSING
is the capital of Michigan, but you've probably heard of the former capital, Detroit, home to the US car industry.

Michigan is called The Great Lakes because four of the five Great Lakes are in parts of Michigan, Lake Superior, Huron, Michigan and Erie. In fact, there are more miles of freshwater shoreline in Michigan than any other state!

With all that freshwater, it's no wonder the state fish is the Brook Trout.

You can see the Northern Lights from north Michigan spots like Lake Superior or Lake Huron.

WORD MATCHES

APPLE	TROUT
AMERICAN	BLOSSOM
GREAT	BRIDGE
MOTOR	LIGHTS
MAKINAC	CITY
LAKE	ROBIN
WHITE	MIDWESTERN
NORTHERN	PINE
BROOK	LAKES
UPPER	SUPERIOR

Michigan is the only state split in two big pieces and connected by the five mile Mackinac Bridge. Can you draw the bridge? It connects between the square dots.

DRAW

- Draw a car at Detroit
- Draw a big civic building at Lansing as this is where the government sits.
- Draw rapids at Grand Rapids (The rapids haven't existed since 1900 when flood walls were installed in the Grand River to remove the rapids)

MINNESOTA

NORTH DAKOTA

SOUTH DAKOTA

WISCONSIN

IOWA

SAINT PAUL
is next to the border with Wisconsin.

CAPITAL CITY: Saint Paul
POPULATION: 5,707,000
REGION: Upper Midwestern / West North Central
ABBREVIATION: MN
STATE FLOWER: Showy Lady's Slipper
STATE TREE: Red Pine
STATE BIRD: The Loon
STATE NICKNAME: The North Star State
NATURAL WONDER: Niagara Cave

Minnesota is also known as the Land of 10,000 lakes, although it has more than that! Somewhere between 11,842 and 14,380 lakes have been counted in Minnesota. Some are shared with other states and Canada and some are very small, so no one can agree on the exact number, but they definitely have 10,000.

The Niagara Cave is an underground wonderland, it's a limestone cave approximately 200 feet (61m) deep with a 60ft waterfall, stalactites, stalagmites and fossils, and you can walk along the water sculpted passageways.

MISSING LETTERS

1. Re_ P_n_
2. N__gar_ Ca_e
3. _ta_ag_ite
4. N_rth _tar S_at_
5. Li_es_one
6. _ossi_
7. S_alac_i_es
8. Rac___n
9. Bo__at
10. _us_rat

CRACK THE CODE

Discover just a few of the 10,000 lakes

_ _ _ _ _ _ _ _ _
8 11 3 25 23 20 11 12 14

_ _ _ _ _ _ _ _ _ _ _ _
20 11 12 14 1 7 21 14 8 3 9 8

_ _ _ _ _ _ _ _ _ _ _ _ _ _
20 11 12 14 22 3 25 25 14 2 9 25 12 11

KEY

1	2	3	4	5	6	7	8	9	10	11	12	13	14	15	16	17	18	19	20	21	22	23	24	25
S	T	I	G	V	D	U	R	O	H	A	K	B	E	C	F	J	Q	Z	L	P	M	Y	W	N

RACCOON MAZE

Raccoons are very popular in Minnesota, as are bobcats, muskrats and red tailed deer.

MISSISSIPPI

CAPITAL CITY: Jackson
POPULATION: 2,950,000
REGION: Southeastern / East South Central
ABBREVIATION: MS
STATE FLOWER & TREE: Magnolia
STATE BIRD: Mockingbird
STATE NICKNAME: The Magnolia State
NATURAL WONDER: Petrified Forest

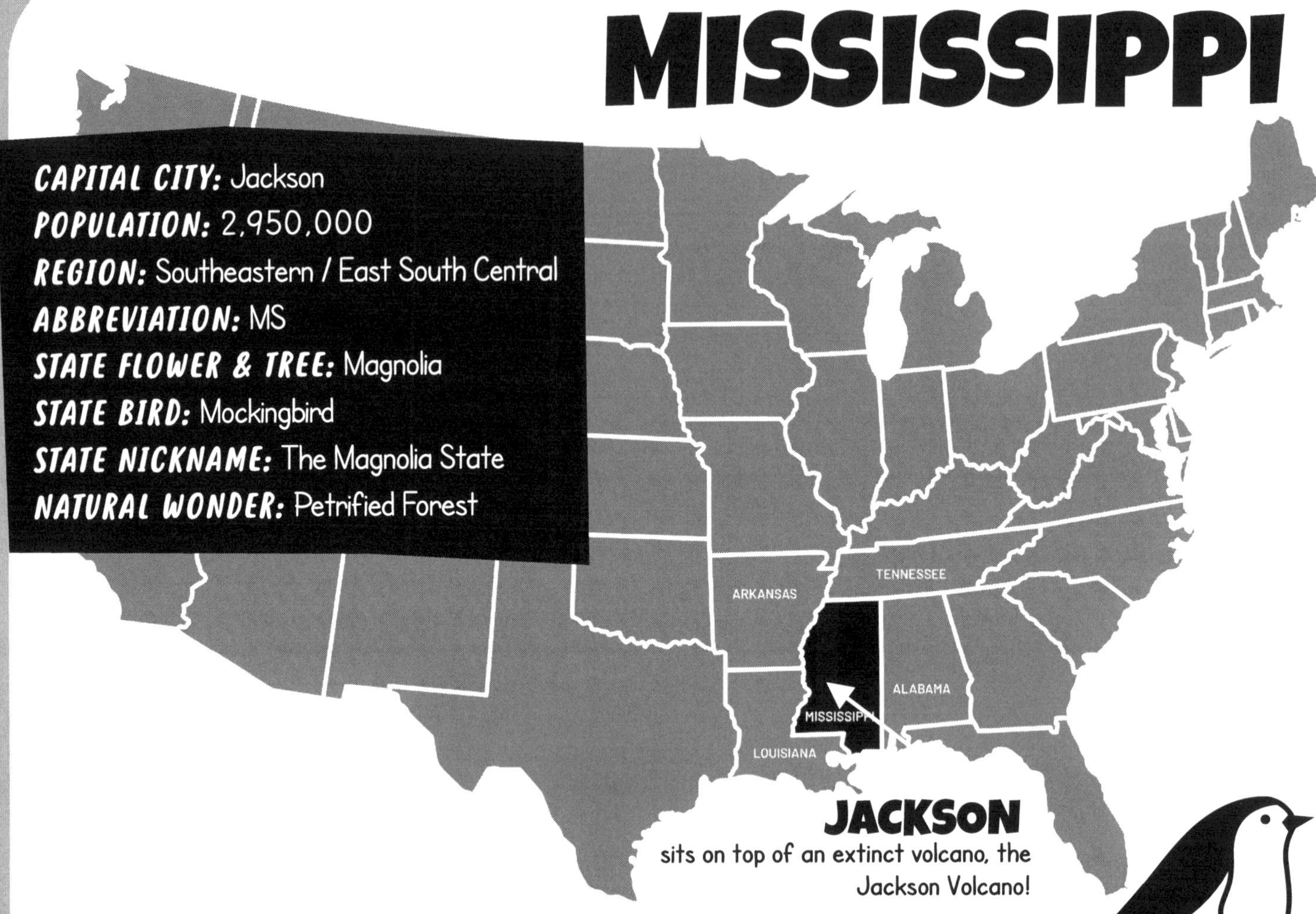

JACKSON sits on top of an extinct volcano, the Jackson Volcano!

The Petrified Forest might sound like something out of Harry Potter, but is definitely not scary! Much like being frozen like the Petrificus Totalus spell, the trees in the Petrified Forest have been fossilized so you can see a 36 million year old log!

The singer, Elvis Presley, King of Rock'n'Roll, is from Mississippi, as is the Queen of talk show TV, Oprah Winfrey.

During Hurricane Katrina in 2005, over 90% of the buildings along the Biloxi - Gulfport coastline were wiped out. The Biloxi Lighthouse survived.

In the 1800's, Mississippi was the countries largest cotton producing state and it still is a major crop in the state. Did you know it grows on trees?

Now, you'll need to know about Universities for the crossword, but we can't just give you the answer, so here are some of the top colleges in the state: University of Mississippi, Mississippi State University, University of Southern Mississippi, Jackson State University and Mississippi College.

CROSSWORD

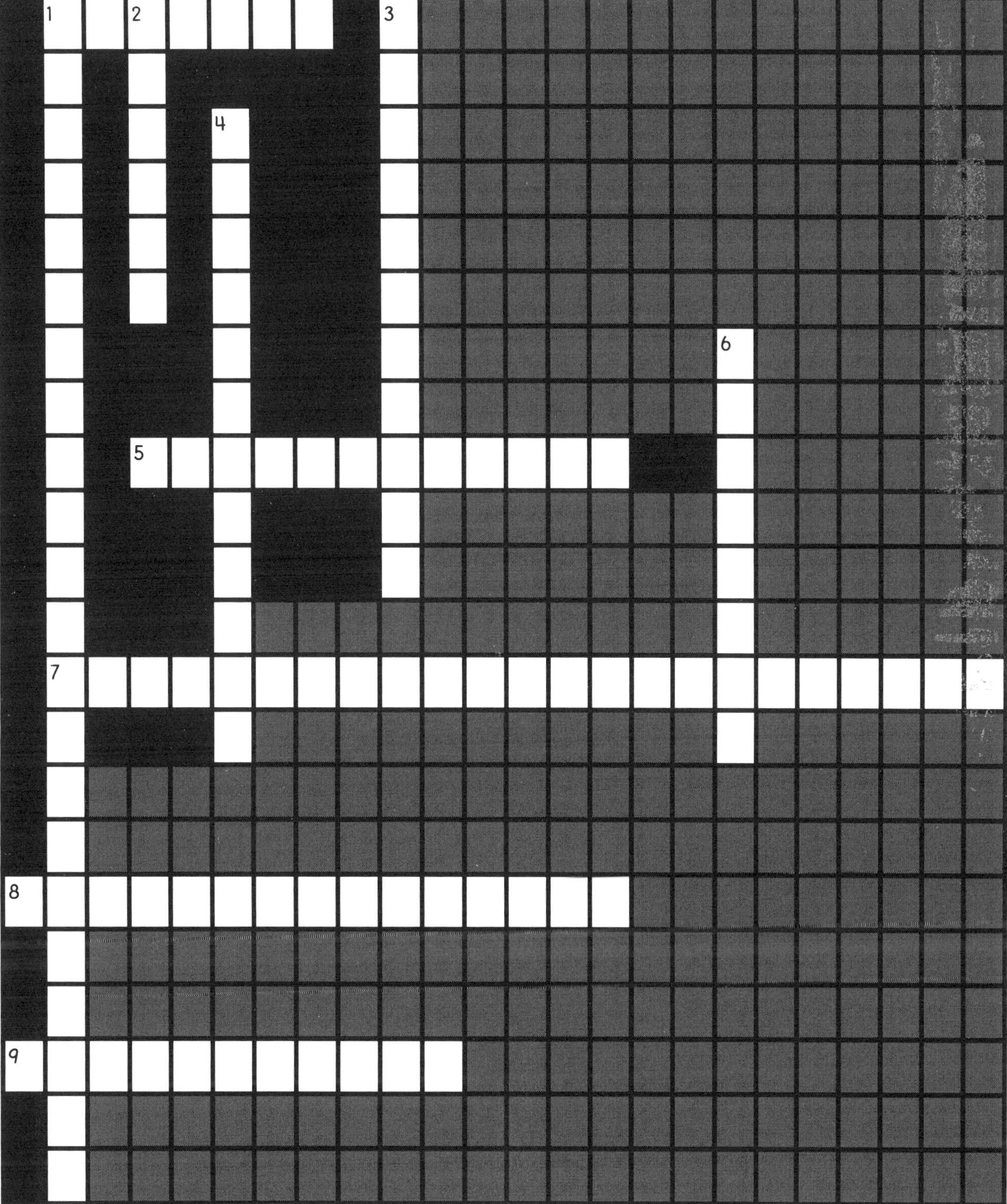

Across

1 Capital city

5 Talk show host

7 College

8 Natural wonder

9 State

Down

1 College

2 State product

3 State bird

4 Singer

6 State flower

CAPITAL CITY: Jefferson City
POPULATION: 6,168,000
REGION: Midwestern / West North Central
ABBREVIATION: MO
STATE FLOWER: White Hawthorn
STATE BIRD: Eastern Bluebird
STATE TREE: Flowering Dogwood
STATE NICKNAME: The Show-Me State
NATURAL WONDER: Marvel Cave

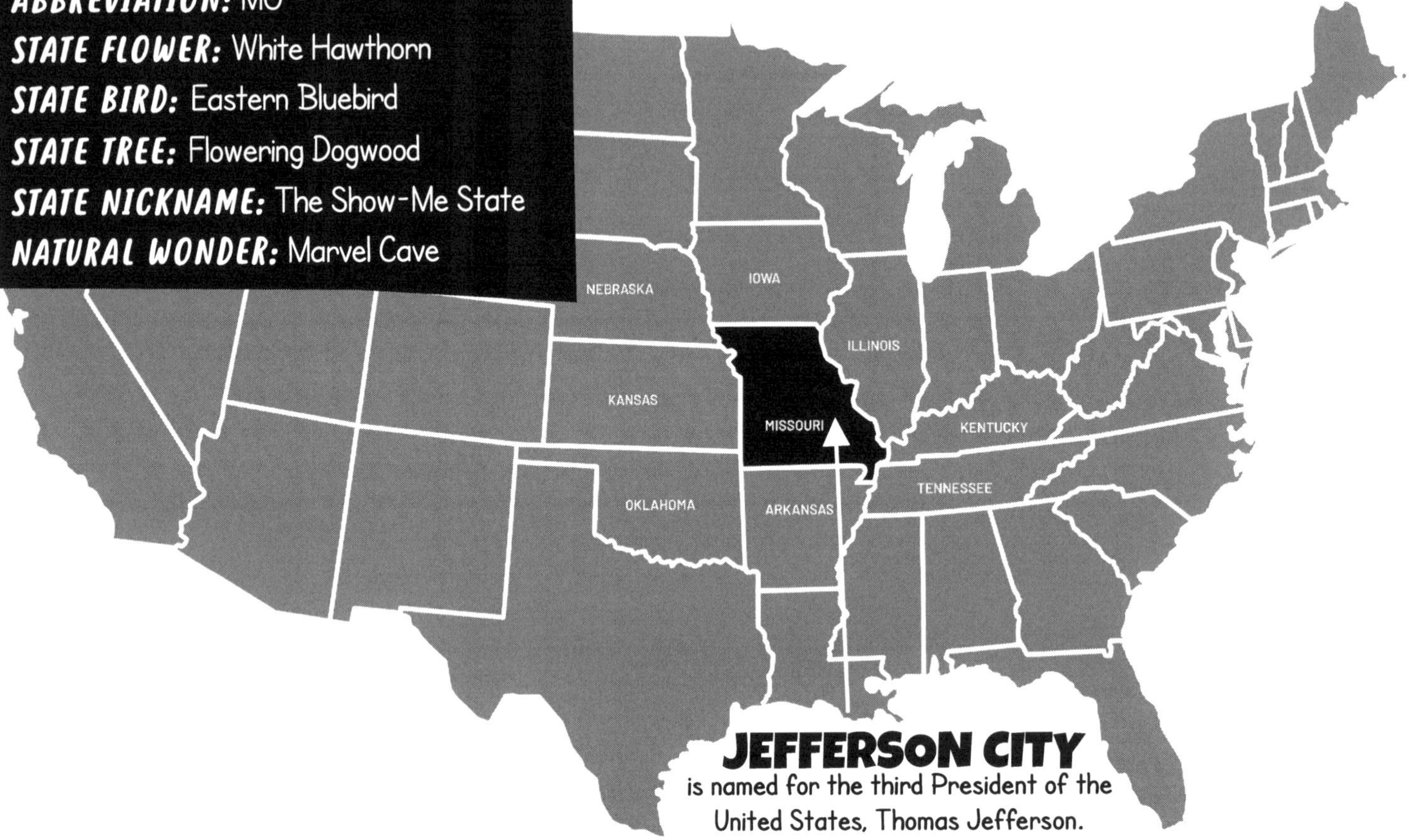

MISSOURI

NEBRASKA
IOWA
ILLINOIS
KANSAS
MISSOURI
KENTUCKY
OKLAHOMA
ARKANSAS
TENNESSEE

JEFFERSON CITY
is named for the third President of the United States, Thomas Jefferson.

Missouri is called the Show Me State, thought to be named after a Missouri representative called Willard Vandiver in 1899 who said "I am from Missouri. You have got to show me." It means that actions speak louder than words.

The largest mammal in North America, the American Bison, calls Missouri home. They can weigh up to 2,200 pounds!

The nation's tallest monument, the Gateway Arch in St Louis, is 630 feet high. It has held the title since it was built in 1965.

Color in this retro tourist poster for Gateway Arch National Park

WORD SEARCH

D	K	A	R	B	R	N	G	A	I	G	C	M	A	B
G	O	L	E	K	N	O	S	N	A	R	B	J	V	E
E	A	B	S	P	R	I	N	G	F	I	E	L	D	F
M	I	S	K	N	D	X	R	Y	V	F	I	H	V	G
P	N	N	F	O	H	N	K	S	S	F	G	V	J	A
A	D	X	C	S	Y	Q	R	A	B	L	U	V	R	C
I	E	B	N	R	B	B	L	O	N	V	T	Z	C	P
B	P	N	Q	E	L	B	A	J	H	S	L	L	B	S
M	E	Y	H	F	U	V	L	B	D	T	A	H	Q	Y
U	N	A	H	F	E	T	H	O	L	E	W	S	Q	P
L	D	C	O	E	B	U	V	Z	M	P	L	A	X	W
O	E	G	Y	J	I	Z	Q	A	K	V	F	G	H	Z
C	N	B	V	P	R	A	R	R	R	F	B	F	Y	O
T	C	Y	B	K	D	F	R	K	R	V	C	X	V	M
X	E	V	H	W	P	A	L	S	W	A	S	Z	G	Z

BBQ
BLUEBIRD
BRANSON
COLUMBIA
HAWTHORN
INDEPENDENCE
JEFFERSON
KANSAS
OZARKS
SPRINGFIELD

MONTANA

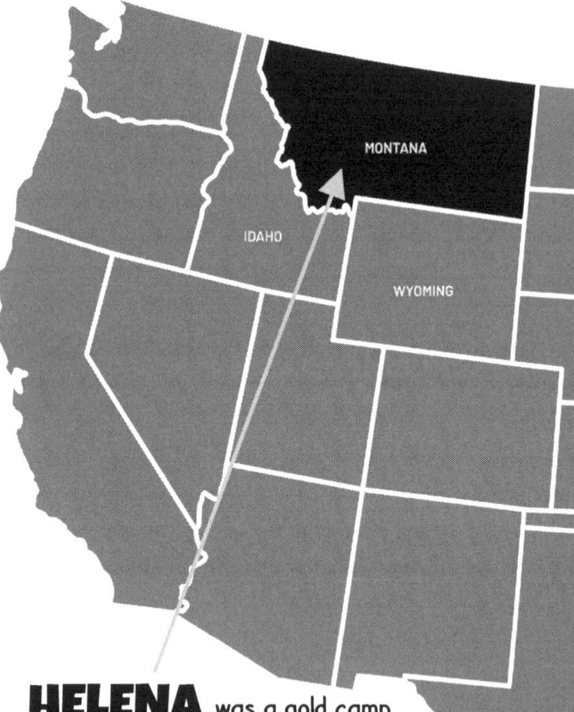

CAPITAL CITY: Helena
POPULATION: 1,104,000
REGION: Western / Mountain States
ABBREVIATION: MT
STATE FLOWER: Bitterroot
STATE TREE: Ponderosa Pine
STATE BIRD: Western Meadowlark
STATE NICKNAME: The Treasure State & Big Sky Country
NATURAL WONDER: Grinnell Glacier

HELENA was a gold camp during the gold rush of 1864 and had roughly 50 millionaires in the area by 1888. That was a lot of millionaires back then!

WORD SCRAMBLE

LGOD _ _ _ _
TOBRRTEOIT _ _ _ _ _ _ _ _ _ _
NAELEH _ _ _ _ _ _
INSAMOUNT _ _ _ _ _ _ _ _ _
LERIVS _ _ _ _ _ _
SRRAUETE _ _ _ _ _ _ _ _
LEIRNMSIOALI _ _ _ _ _ _ _ _ _ _ _ _
ARBES _ _ _ _ _
SBOIN _ _ _ _ _
EWVSOL _ _ _ _ _ _

Montana's name comes from the Spanish word montaña, which is a fancy way of saying 'mountainous.' That's because there are a lot of mountains in this state, a whopping 300 peaks that are taller than 9,600 feet!

The Treasure State nickname comes from the mining of gold and silver from the mountains in the 1800's.

Those infamous mountains are home to grizzly and black bears, gray wolves and bison.

COLOR ME IN!

MONTANA MAZE

Can you make it from the south to the north?

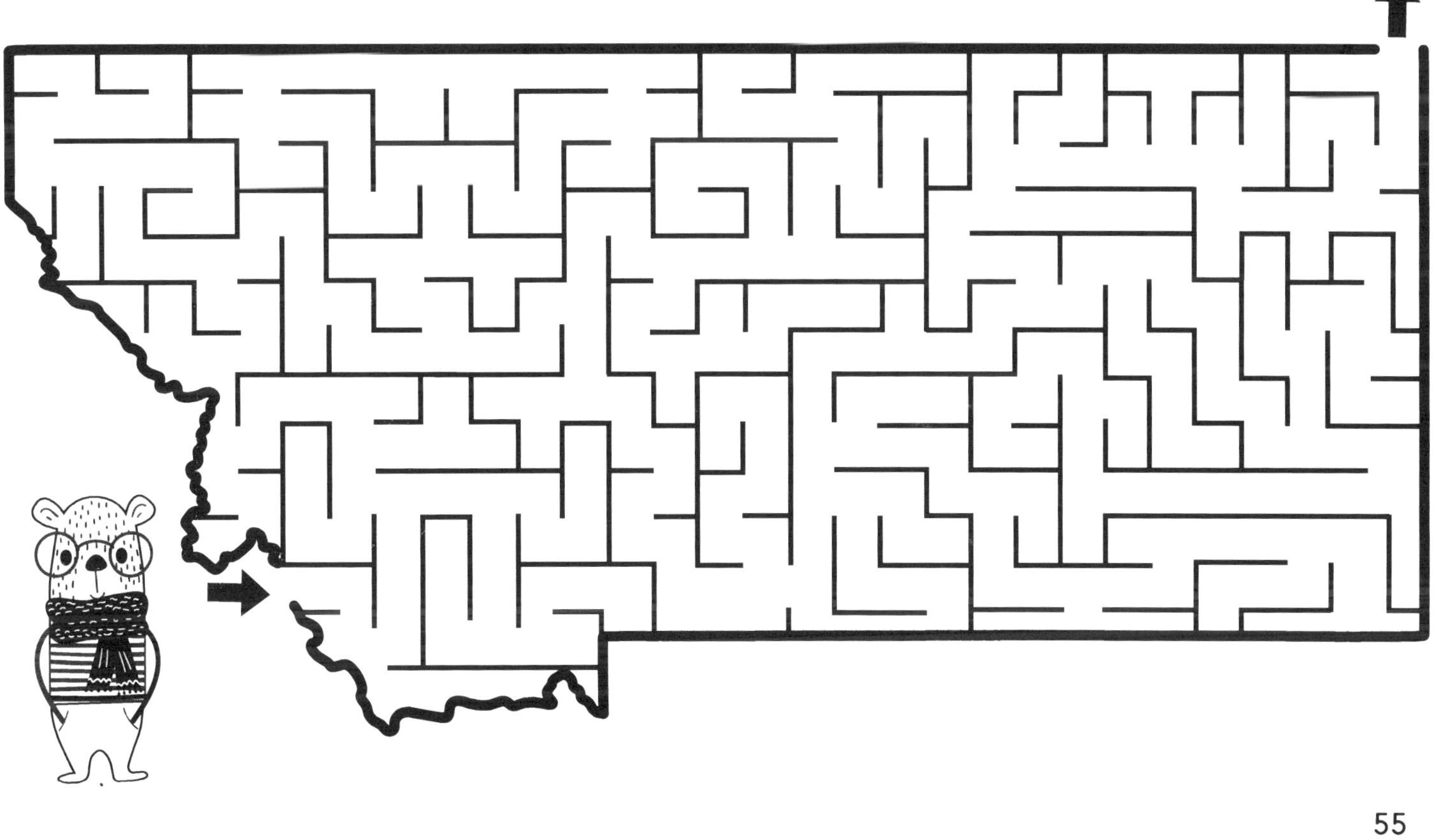

NEBRASKA

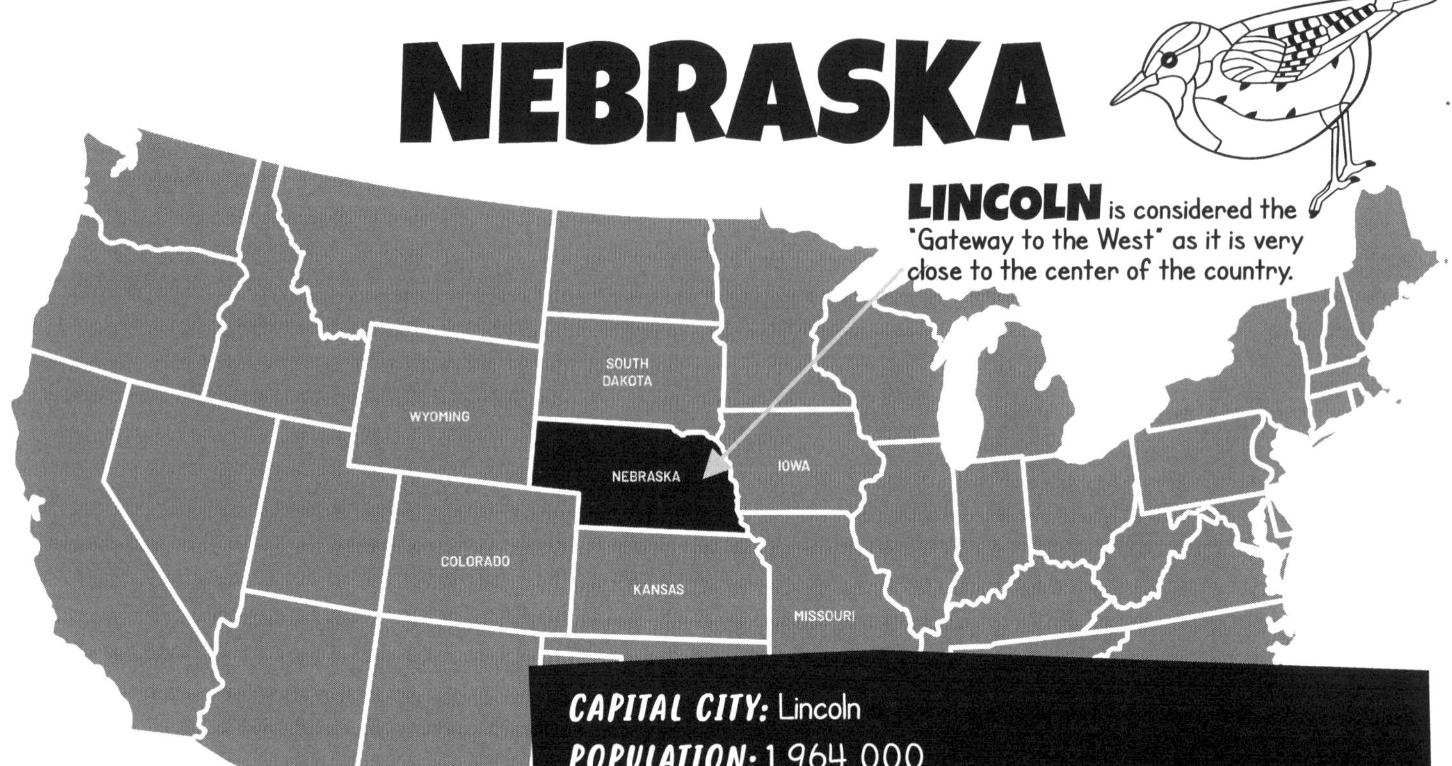

LINCOLN is considered the "Gateway to the West" as it is very close to the center of the country.

CAPITAL CITY: Lincoln
POPULATION: 1,964,000
REGION: Midwestern / West North Central
ABBREVIATION: NE
STATE FLOWER: Goldenrod
STATE TREE: Eastern Cottonwood
STATE BIRD: Western Meadowlark
STATE NICKNAME: The Tree Planters' State & Cornhusker State
NATURAL WONDER: Ashfall Fossil Beds

Nebraska means "flat water" in Native American, referring to the Platte River which runs through the state.

Scotts Bluff is a landmark to Native Americans and rises 800 feet above the Platte River.

About 12 million years ago there was a volcanic event that rocked the land and caused some animals, like saber-toothed deer, raccoon dogs and giraffe-like camels to go extinct. But their fossilized remains have been preserved like secret treasures at the Ashfall Fossil Beds in northeastern Nebraska.

WORD MATCHES

WESTERN	STATE
FOSSIL	FOSSIL
CORNHUSKER	MEADOWLARK
SCOTTS	RIVER
PLATTE	COTTONWOOD
FLAT	BEDS
EASTERN	BLUFF
ASHFALL	WATER

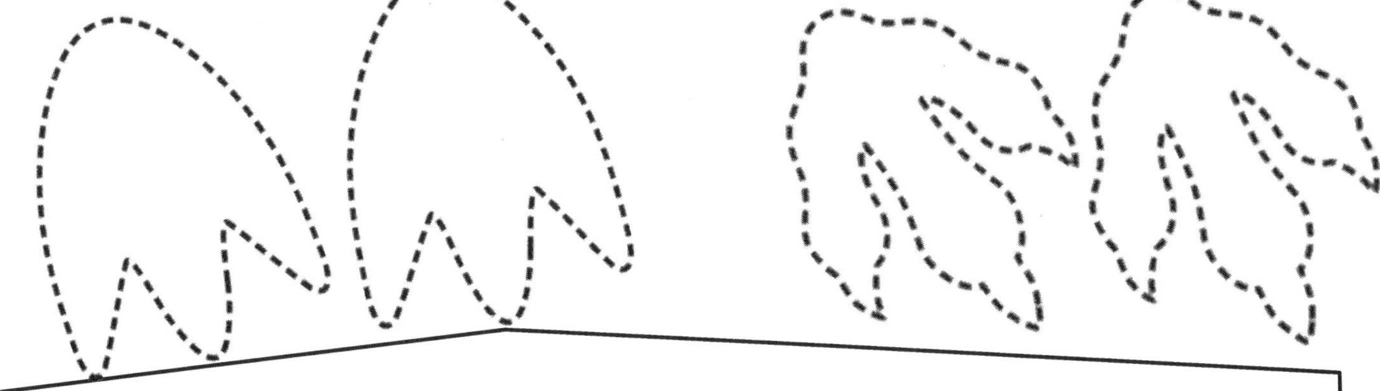

CRACK THE CODE

Uncover extinct animals from 12 million years ago.

_ _ _ _ _ _ _   _ _ _ _
9 12 11 11 18 18 19   21 18 10 4

_ _ _ _ _ - _ _ _ _ _   _ _ _ _
4 12 5 20 9 - 23 18 18 23 17   21 20 20 9

_ _ _ _ _ _ _   _ _ _ _ _ _
10 15 9 12 1 1 20   11 12 3 20 6 4

KEY

1	2	3	4	5	6	7	8	9	10	11	12	13	14	15	16	17	18	19	20	21	22	23	24	25
F	W	M	S	B	L	U	X	R	G	C	A	K	Y	I	J	H	O	N	E	D	Q	T	V	Z

NEVADA

CAPITAL CITY: Carson City
POPULATION: 3,144,000
REGION: Western / Mountain States
ABBREVIATION: NV
STATE FLOWER: Mayflower
STATE BIRD: Sagebrush
STATE TREE: Flowering Bristlecone Pine & Single Leaf Piñon
STATE NICKNAME: The Silver State
NATURAL WONDER: Valley of Fire State Park

CARSON CITY is named after mountain man Kit Carson. A mountain man is an explorer who lives off the wilderness and makes a living hunting and trapping, a bit like Bear Grylls if he traded the animals he killed and caught.

Nevada is home to Las Vegas, the unofficial Entertainment Capital of the World. It has luxurious casinos, live performances at any time of day and bright lights.

The name Nevada comes from the Spanish word nieve, which means snow-capped, referring to the Sierra Nevada mountain range that runs along the Western border with California.

There is also desert in Nevada, the Mojave Desert crosses from California and within it lives rattlesnakes and desert tortoises. Nevada also has the largest population of wild horses.

MISSING LETTERS

1. L_s V__as
2. _ilver _t_t_
3. Ma__lo_er
4. S__eb_u__
5. K_t C__s_n
6. S_e__a Ne_a_a
7. _a__le_na_e
8. T__toi__
9. Va__ey o_ _ir_
10. Wi__ Ho__es

DOT TO DOT

40 1 41 2 39 3 8 36 6 5 38 35 7 10 4 12 37 9 11 24 13 34 29 25 14 23 19 30 33 26 15 22 18 28 20 32 17 31 27 21 16

Color in this postcard and then label the city. Make it very bright, if you have neon colors use those!

NEW HAMPSHIRE

CONCORD State House is America's oldest capital city building.

VERMONT
MAINE
NEW HAMPSHIRE
MASSACHUSETTS

CAPITAL CITY: Concord
POPULATION: 1,389,000
REGION: Northeastern / New England
ABBREVIATION: NH
STATE FLOWER: Purple Lilac
STATE TREE: White Burch
STATE BIRD: Purple Finch
STATE NICKNAME: The Granite State
NATURAL WONDER: The Flume Gorge

New Hampshire was the first colony to declare its independence from Great Britain in 1766. It had a motto to go with this "Live Free or Die" that is still the official motto.

As you'd expect from a state called "The Granite State", NH has a *deep* history in granite quarries and mining.

The first public library in the United States was opened in Peterborough, NH in 1833.

COLOR A QUARTER

Imagine if a quarter wasn't silver. Color this the colors you want it to be.

NEW HAMPSHIRE CITY SEARCH

K	M	X	P	F	Z	E	L	K	W	X	R	C	V	N
C	R	V	L	O	N	D	O	N	D	E	R	R	Y	M
Y	Y	K	T	J	D	K	K	Z	V	B	P	T	A	K
S	T	R	C	L	H	R	S	A	N	B	T	N	L	T
A	R	R	R	A	H	U	D	S	O	N	C	V	O	S
L	K	E	U	E	M	Y	H	P	Q	H	K	F	A	X
E	N	U	V	L	D	I	F	F	E	A	E	N	H	W
M	S	V	F	O	G	O	R	S	D	O	O	T	Q	S
Q	R	H	B	V	D	P	T	R	E	R	D	F	A	L
S	O	N	Y	N	R	E	M	O	E	C	V	H	J	Y
V	A	Y	C	R	R	S	A	N	U	M	C	E	A	V
F	A	N	M	W	N	X	F	R	Q	H	N	R	C	T
I	M	N	A	S	H	U	A	Z	Z	O	D	A	X	H
P	X	B	I	I	P	S	C	O	N	C	O	R	D	Z
H	L	Q	H	G	R	O	C	H	E	S	T	E	R	A

CONCORD
DERRY
DOVER
HUDSON
LONDONDERRY

MANCHESTER
MERRIMACK
NASHUA
ROCHESTER
SALEM

NEW JERSEY

TRENTON was the capital of the United States for 54 days in 1784.

CAPITAL CITY: Trenton
POPULATION: 9,260,000
REGION: Northeast / Mid-Atlantic
ABBREVIATION: NJ
STATE FLOWER: Violet
STATE TREE: Northern Red Oak
STATE BIRD: American Goldfinch
STATE NICKNAME: The Garden State
NATURAL WONDER: Sterling Hill Mine

New Jersey is often referred to as the Garden State because of its rich agricultural history and abundance of gardens and farmland.

This state is famous for boardwalks, with the earliest built in 1870 in Atlantic City. The boardwalks provide entertainment, shopping and dining.

Thomas Edison, the inventor of the lightbulb (and heaps of other things) had his lab in this state.

The street names on Monopoly are named after the streets of Atlantic City.

New Jersey has a state dance! The popular folk dance, square dancing is the state dance.

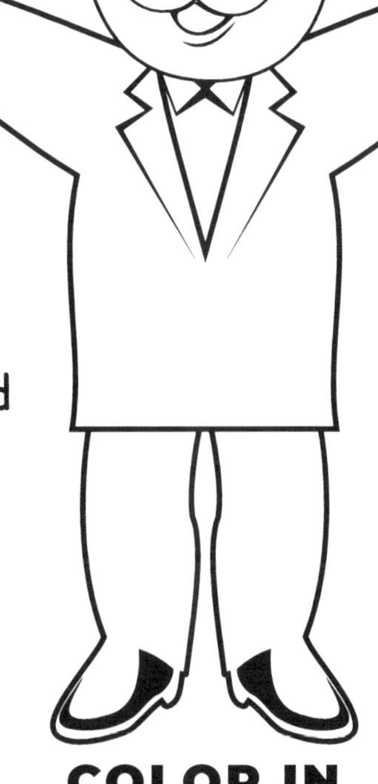

COLOR IN
The Monopoly Man

CROSSWORD

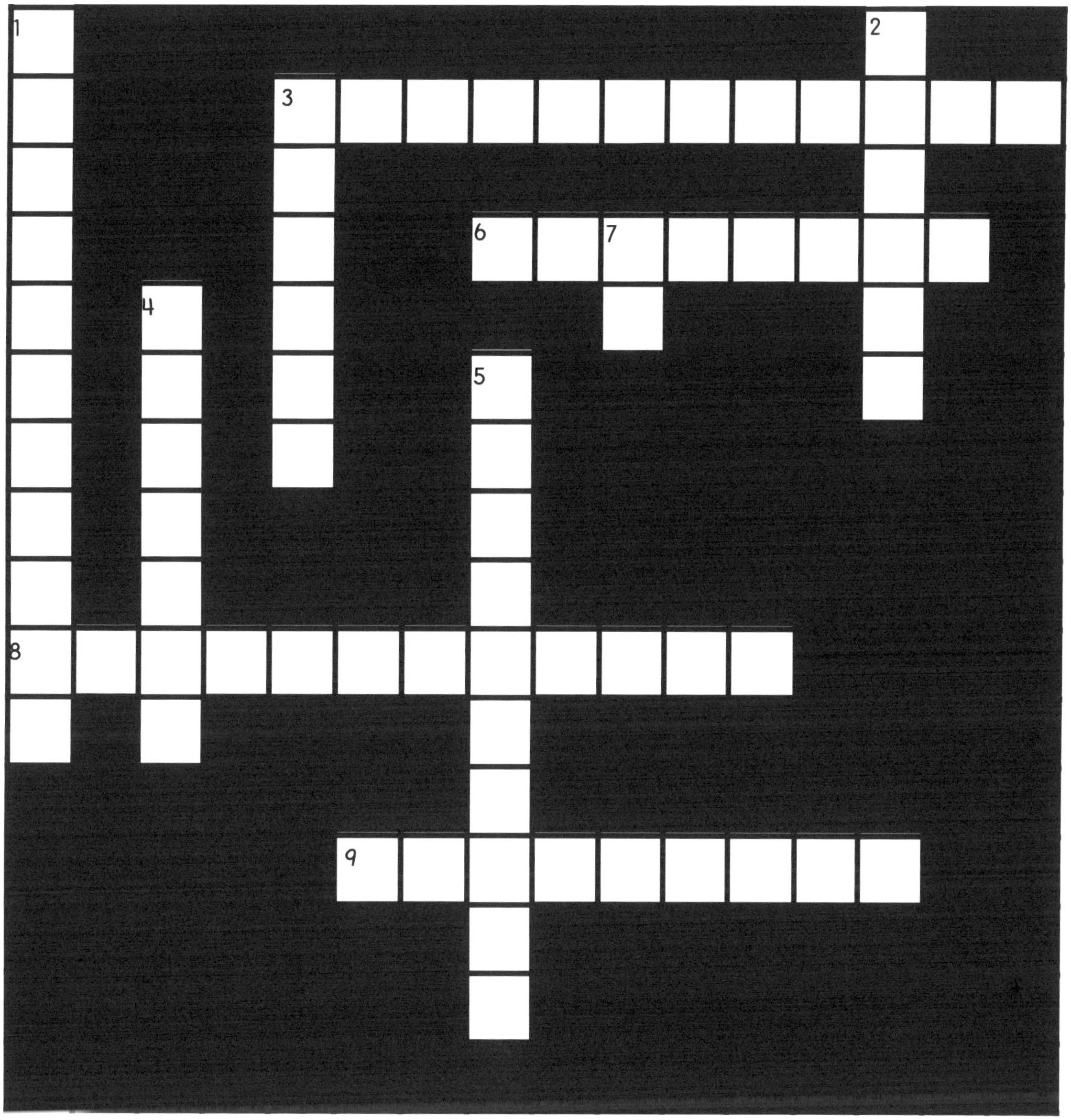

Across

3. Natural wonder location
6. The street names in this game are based in Atlantic city
8. Inventor of the light bulb
9. State bird

Down

1. State nickname
2. State flower
3. State dance is called
4. Capital city
5. Famous entertainment areas
7. State abbreviation

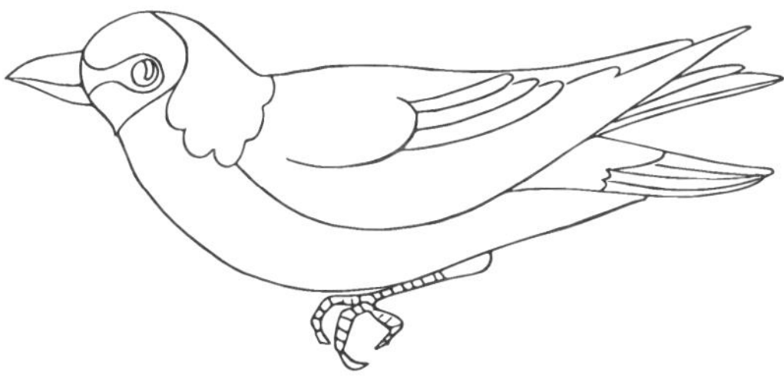

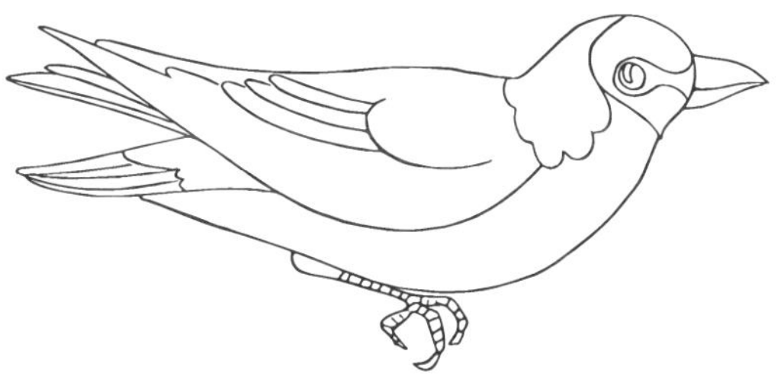

NEW MEXICO

UTAH
COLORADO
ARIZONA
NEW MEXICO
OKLAHOMA
TEXAS

CAPITAL CITY: Santa Fe
POPULATION: 2,116,000
REGION: Southwest / Mountain States
ABBREVIATION: NM
STATE FLOWER: Yucca
STATE TREE: Piñon pine
STATE BIRD: Greater Roadrunner
STATE NICKNAME: Land of Enchantment
NATURAL WONDER: Valles Caldera (Super Volcano)

SANTA FE should be called "Sunny Fe" as it gets about 320 sunny days a year!

In south western New Mexico is White Sands National Monument, the world's largest field of sand dunes made of gypsum sand (which is pretty rare as gypsum sand is water soluble!).

New Mexico is not just desert, the state has varied landscapes including grasslands and snow capped mountains.

WORD SCRAMBLE

YNSNU _ _ _ _ _

ACYUC _ _ _ _ _

PUYGMS _ _ _ _ _ _

NSDA _ _ _ _

OMITNUNA _ _ _ _ _ _ _ _

LSRSDAANG _ _ _ _ _ _ _ _ _

SIANLE _ _ _ _ _ _

EWLLRSO _ _ _ _ _ _ _

RETDSE _ _ _ _ _ _

EODNRRURNA _ _ _ _ _ _ _ _ _ _

If you've heard of aliens, you may have also heard of a city called Roswell, New Mexico, that is allegedly the site of a UFO crash in 1947. Of course there is a UFO museum there.

NEW MEXICO MAZE

Can you navigate from the top of the spacecraft to the bottom?

NEW YORK

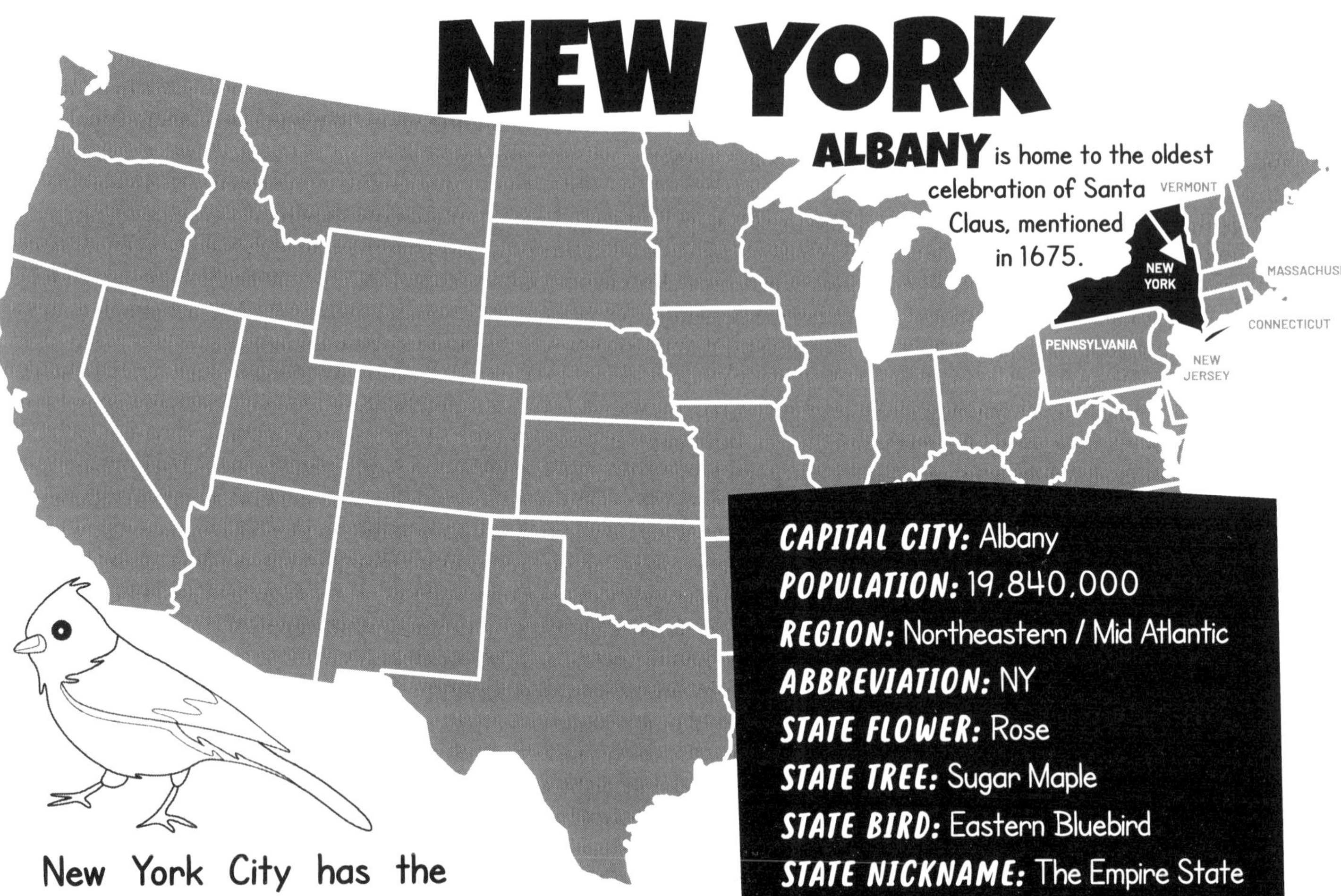

ALBANY is home to the oldest celebration of Santa Claus, mentioned in 1675.

CAPITAL CITY: Albany
POPULATION: 19,840,000
REGION: Northeastern / Mid Atlantic
ABBREVIATION: NY
STATE FLOWER: Rose
STATE TREE: Sugar Maple
STATE BIRD: Eastern Bluebird
STATE NICKNAME: The Empire State
NATURAL WONDER: Niagara Falls

New York City has the biggest population of any city in the USA, with 8.5 million residents. Also in the city that never sleeps is 722 miles of subway track and Ellis Island, where 12 million immigrants arrived between 1892 and 1924.

Central Park is in the heart of New York City and is a massive urban park with a zoo.

In northern New York state, are the Finger Lakes, a group of 11 long narrow lakes that look like fingers from the air. Also in this region is the Erie Canal, which led to New York becoming the main commercial city in the USA. This was completed in 1825.

WORD MATCHES

NIAGARA	STATION
EMPIRE	FALLS
SUGAR	BLUEBIRD
ELLIS	MAPLE
CENTRAL	AMSTERDAM
FINGER	STATE
ERIE	ISLAND
EASTERN	LAKES
NEW	CANAL
RAILWAY	PARK

New York city used to be called New Amsterdam, this was after the Dutch decided to claim it in the 1600s.

Grand Central Terminal in Manhattan is the largest railway station in the world .

TAXI!

There are over 13,000 taxis in New York City, making it the city with the most taxis in the United States.

You are sightseeing for the day. Draw a taxi at each destination.

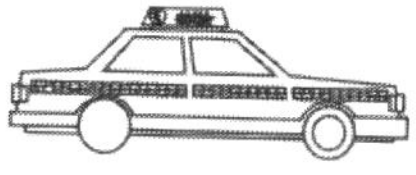

1. Metropolitan Museum
2. Times Square
3. Madison Square Garden
4. Brooklyn Bridge
5. One World Trade Center

Feel free to join them up and add other attractions you would like to visit!

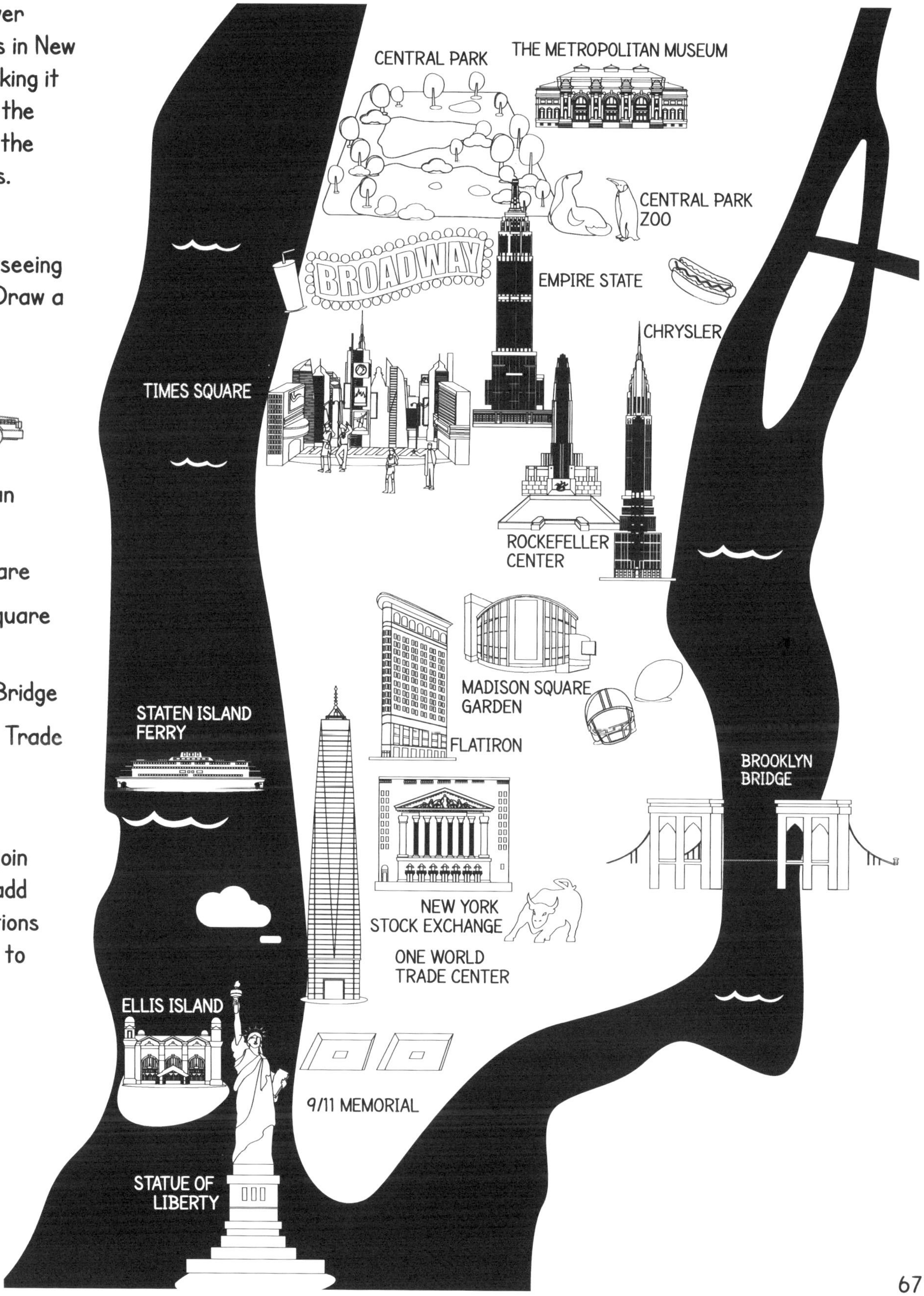

CENTRAL PARK

THE METROPOLITAN MUSEUM

CENTRAL PARK ZOO

BROADWAY

EMPIRE STATE

CHRYSLER

TIMES SQUARE

ROCKEFELLER CENTER

MADISON SQUARE GARDEN

FLATIRON

STATEN ISLAND FERRY

BROOKLYN BRIDGE

NEW YORK STOCK EXCHANGE

ONE WORLD TRADE CENTER

ELLIS ISLAND

9/11 MEMORIAL

STATUE OF LIBERTY

NORTH CAROLINA

CAPITAL CITY: Raleigh
POPULATION: 10,550,000
REGION: Southeastern / South Atlantic
ABBREVIATION: NC
STATE FLOWER: Dogwood
STATE TREE: Pine
STATE BIRD: Northern Cardinal
STATE NICKNAME: Old North State & Tar Heel State
NATURAL WONDER: Jockey's Ridge

The first powered airplane flight by the Wright Brothers took off from Kitty Hawk, NC.

More than half of North Carolina is covered by forests, and this is a big reason why the state is one of the biggest makers of furniture in the USA.

The eastern region of North Carolina is called the coastal plain and then further east in the Atlantic Ocean are the Outer Banks, a group of barrier islands. These islands protect the coastal mainland from raging waves and storms.

MISSING LETTERS

1. Ki_ _y Haw_
2. D_ _w_ _d
3. _oc_e_'s Ri_ _e
4. Ta_ H_ _l _t_te
5. _ur_i_ur_
6. O_ _ Tr_ _s
7. Coa_ _al _la_ _
8. _u_er B_ _ks
9. Ba_ _ier _s_an_s
10. _ai_ _an_

DOT TO DOT

NORTH DAKOTA

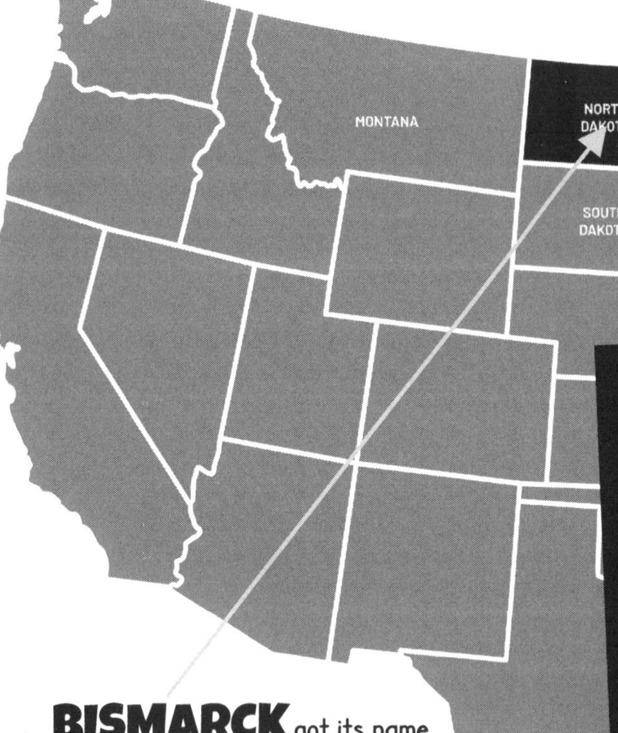

CAPITAL CITY: Bismarck
POPULATION: 780,000
REGION: Upper Midwest / West North Central
ABBREVIATION: ND
STATE FLOWER: Wild Prairie Rose
STATE TREE: American Elm
STATE BIRD: Western Meadowlark
STATE NICKNAME: Peace Garden State
NATURAL WONDER: Cannonball Concretions Pullout

BISMARCK got its name to honor the German Chancellor, Otto Von Bismarck, in the hope of attracting German investment in the railway.

North Dakota shares a border with Canada, which it also shares an International Peace Garden with. This is a botanic garden in the Turtle Mountains which is a monument to friendship and cooperation between the USA and Canada.

North Dakota is the biggest producer of honey in the US. As well as having loads of bees, the state also has a lot of lakes and rivers that provide excellent fishing.

30% of the population in North Dakota is of Scandinavian ancestry, mostly Norwegian. This is from immigrants who arrived from 1870 to 1920.

COLOR THE DALA HORSE

A Dala horse is a Swedish traditional carved, painted wooden statue of a horse. Use bright colors like green and orange.

WORD SEARCH

T	J	E	K	W	T	V	H	A	F	L	P	S	S	P
B	X	P	I	P	U	T	O	M	I	H	P	C	N	O
X	D	S	W	M	R	L	N	B	S	A	I	A	O	E
U	P	B	E	H	T	O	E	U	H	L	F	N	B	Z
U	G	P	I	A	L	I	Y	F	I	Q	S	D	G	T
I	U	N	S	S	E	L	F	F	N	C	R	I	M	A
O	T	H	V	U	M	L	C	A	G	P	O	N	J	Z
G	P	Q	Z	C	O	A	H	L	K	F	T	A	K	S
R	T	M	O	B	U	M	R	O	N	V	O	V	Z	R
A	F	A	M	Y	N	K	O	K	D	L	U	I	J	E
F	I	L	D	M	T	K	I	T	D	Z	E	A	O	V
R	C	T	W	H	A	W	H	V	P	E	S	N	B	I
D	B	E	W	A	I	W	M	Q	W	P	V	E	G	R
Y	Q	P	J	E	N	G	M	V	N	N	E	L	S	S
C	W	Y	D	N	S	O	D	Y	Q	X	D	P	L	X

BISMARK
BUFFALO
FARGO
FISHING
HONEY
OIL
RIVERS
SCANDINAVIAN
TURTLE MOUNTAINS

OHIO

COLUMBUS is known for being the "Biggest Small Town in America".

CAPITAL CITY: Columbus
POPULATION: 11,780,000
REGION: Northeastern / East North Central
ABBREVIATION: OH
STATE FLOWER: Carnation
STATE TREE: Ohio Buckeye
STATE BIRD: Cardinal
STATE NICKNAME: The Buckeye State
NATURAL WONDER: Kelleys Island Glacial Grooves

The Ohio Buckeye is a very common tree in the state, with nuts that look like a deer's eye, hence the name "Buck Eye" (as in buck = male deer).

The state is home to the Till Plains in the west that is the start of America's corn belt, including Illinois, Indiana, Michigan, Nebraska, Minnesota and Missouri.

The three largest cities in Ohio all begin with the letter C, Columbus, Cleveland and Cincinnati.

Whilst the first flight for the Wright Brothers took off from Kitty Hawk, NC, they conducted most of their early experiments and created the first airplane in Dayton, OH which is where they grew up.

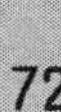

CROSSWORD

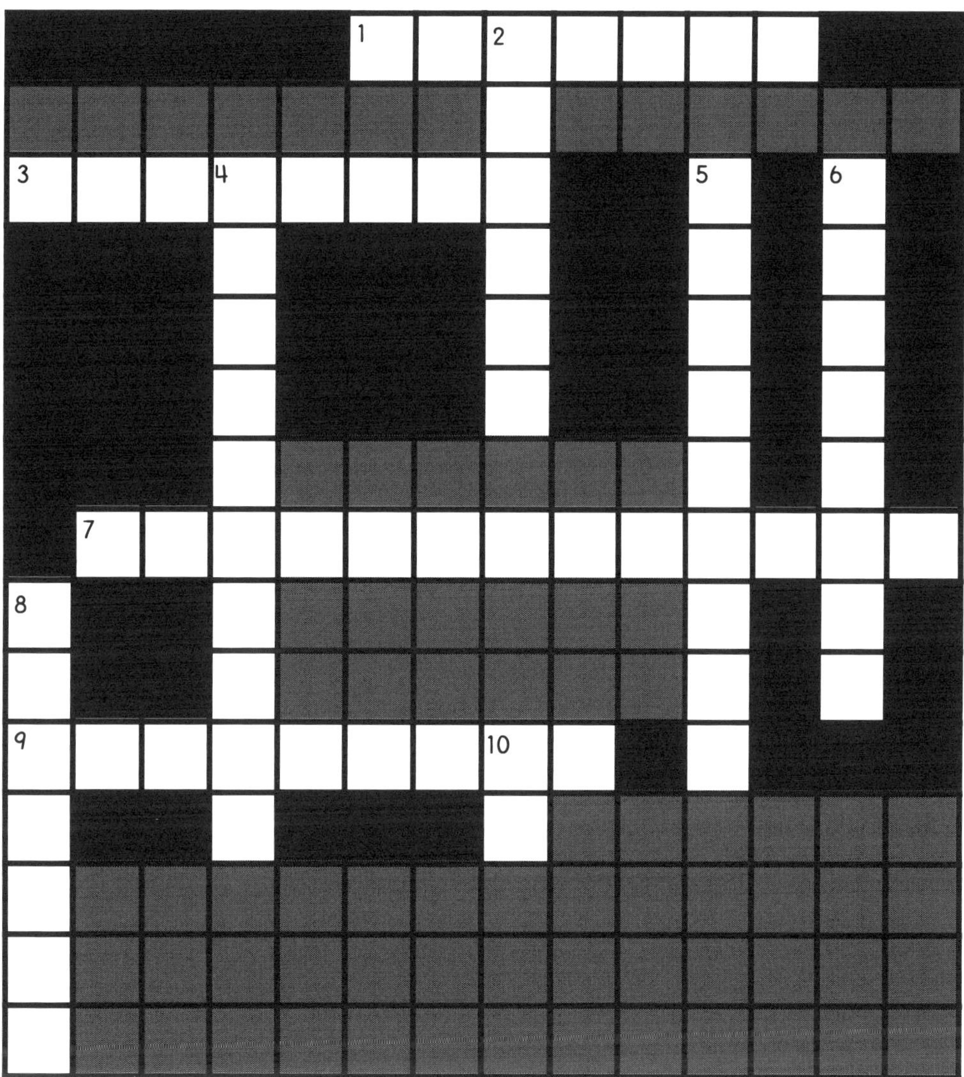

Across

1. Neighboring state to the west
3. Neighboring state to the south
7. Location of natural wonder
9. State flower

Down

2. City where the Wright Brothers lived
4. The region at the start of the Corn Belt
5. One of the biggest cities beginning with C
6. State bird
8. Name for male deer +eye
10. State abbreviation

OKLAHOMA

CAPITAL CITY: Oklahoma City
POPULATION: 3,987,000
REGION: Southwest / West South Central
ABBREVIATION: OK
STATE FLOWER: Oklahoma Rose
STATE TREE: Eastern Redbud
STATE BIRD: Scissor-tailed Flycatcher
STATE NICKNAME: The Sooner State
NATURAL WONDER: Great Salt Plains

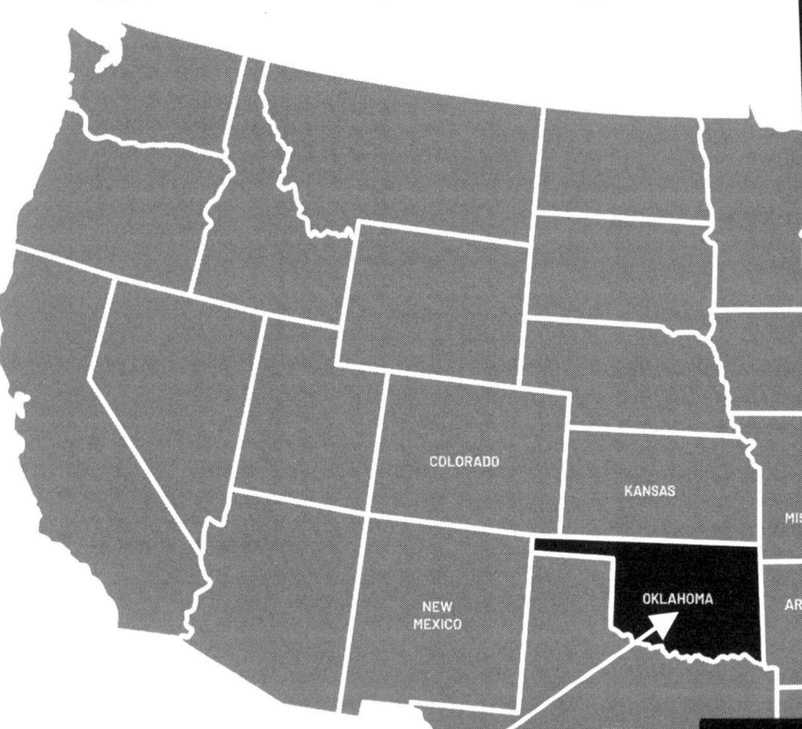

OKLAHOMA CITY

is one of only two states that include the state's name as part of the city's name. The other is Indianapolis.

In south-central Oklahoma is one of North America's oldest ranges, the Arbuckle Mountains which are 1.3 billions years old!

Tulsa is the second biggest city in Oklahoma and used to be known as "Oil Capital of the World". Two thirds of the Oklahoma population live in Oklahoma City and Tulsa.

OK is called the Sooner State because early settlers arrived sooner than they were supposed to. They just couldn't wait!

WORD SCRAMBLE

DUEBRD _ _ _ _ _ _

YLTHCFCRAE _ _ _ _ _ _ _ _ _ _

RKLBUACE _ _ _ _ _ _ _ _

UTSAL _ _ _ _ _

ILO _ _ _

RSNOOE TESAT _ _ _ _ _ _ _ _ _ _ _ _

SOER _ _ _ _

TLAS LAPNIS _ _ _ _ _ _ _ _ _ _ _

IBNSO _ _ _ _ _

AHITCIW _ _ _ _ _ _ _

The Bison (Buffalo) is the official state animal and in the Wichita Mountains they roam freely.

CRACK THE CODE

Discover the counties where the Arbuckle Mountains lie.

__ __ __ __ __ __ __ __
9 15 25 13 15 13 15 3

__ __ __ __ __ __
3 22 12 13 20 12

__ __ __ __ __ __ __ __
7 15 23 25 4 13 15 25

__ __ __ __ __ __
2 8 12 12 22 11

KEY

1	2	3	4	5	6	7	8	9	10	11	12	13	14	15	16	17	18	19	20	21	22	23	24	25
X	M	C	S	Q	B	J	U	P	Z	Y	R	T	G	O	F	W	L	D	E	K	A	H	I	N

OREGON

WASHINGTON
OREGON
IDAHO
NEVADA
CALIFORNIA

CAPITAL CITY: Salem
POPULATION: 4,246,000
REGION: Western / Pacific Northwest
ABBREVIATION: OR
STATE FLOWER: Oregon Grape
STATE TREE: Douglas Fir
STATE BIRD: Western Meadowlark
STATE NICKNAME: Beaver State
NATURAL WONDER: Crater Lake

SALEM

is the nicknamed the "Cherry City". Since 1847 Salem has had successful cherry orchards, some say the finest in the country.

Crater Lake is the deepest lake in the United States with a depth of 1,943 feet. In contrast to the deepest lake, Oregon is also home to the smallest park, Mill Ends Park, which is on a median strip in Portland and is only a 2ft circle!

Oregon's state animal is the beaver and they are very common, other common animals in the state are elks, gray wolves, burrowing owls and snowy plovers.

Like cheese? Oregon has the largest cheese factory in the world, the Tillamook Cheese Factory.

WORD MATCHES

DOUGLAS	LAKE
OREGON	STATE
WESTERN	PLOVER
BEAVER	PARK
CRATER	FIR
GRAY	FACTORY
SNOWY	OWLS
MILL ENDS	GRAPE
CHEESE	MEADOWLARK
BURROWING	WOLVES

Mill Ends Park was created by a journalist as a joke. Dick Fagan started writing a column about the goings-on in the "park" (remember it is a 2 ft circle on a median strip) in 1946 and called it Mill Ends.

He wrote about seeing a leprechaun digging a hole in the park and how a family of leprechaun's had moved in. A swimming pool for butterflies was added and a miniature ferris wheel.

You have taken over Dick Fagan's Mill Ends column. Write a headline, then a wild story about that is totally unbelievable. You might want to draw in some pictures to the right, or use those spaces between the stars to write a sizzling summary to draw readers into your column.

PENNSYLVANIA

CAPITAL CITY: Harrisburg
POPULATION: 12,960,000
REGION: Northeast / Mid-Atlantic
ABBREVIATION: PA
STATE FLOWER: Mountain Laurel
STATE TREE: Eastern Hemlock
STATE BIRD: Ruffed Grouse
STATE NICKNAME: The Keystone State
NATURAL WONDER: Pine Creek Gorge - PA Grand Canyon

HARRISBURG was chosen as the capital due to its location being near the middle of the state. You might think Philadelphia is the capital, it has a larger population, but is located in the southeastern corner so not very convenient when you had to travel by horse and carriage in the 1700 and 1800's!

The first settlers may have been in Pennsylvania 15,000 years ago and they left a clue called the Meadowcroft Rockshelter. Tools and pottery were discovered within the shelter.

Pennsylvania became the second US state in 1787. It is called the Keystone State because it is the keystone of American values and culture.

This state's mammals include black bears, elk, white-tailed deer and red foxes.

Color in this basketball logo

DOT TO DOT

MISSING LETTERS

1. Ke_s_one __a_e
2. _oun_ain Lau___
3. _lac_ B__rs
4. P_ila_el_hia
5. Me__ow_ra_t Ro__she__er
6. _ine _ree_ _or_e
7. Re_ _o_es
8. Ha__isbu_g
9. Ru__ed _ro_se
10. _enn__l_a_ia

RHODE ISLAND

CAPITAL CITY: Providence
POPULATION: 1,096,000
REGION: Northeastern / New England
ABBREVIATION: RI
STATE FLOWER: Violet
STATE TREE: Red Maple
STATE BIRD: Rhode Island Red Chicken
STATE NICKNAME: The Ocean State
NATURAL WONDER: Block Island

PROVIDENCE

Has the most coffee and donut shops per person in the entire country!

MASSACHUSETTS
RHODE ISLAND
CONNECTICUT

Rhode Island is the smallest US State at 1,214 square miles. It is nicknamed the Ocean State because it has more than 400 miles of coastline and everywhere in the state is less than a half hour drive to the sea!

Speaking of coastline, Rhode Island shares a state water border with New York.

The first "official" circus in the United States was in Newport, RI in 1774. It was mostly horse riding displays in a specially built riding academy.

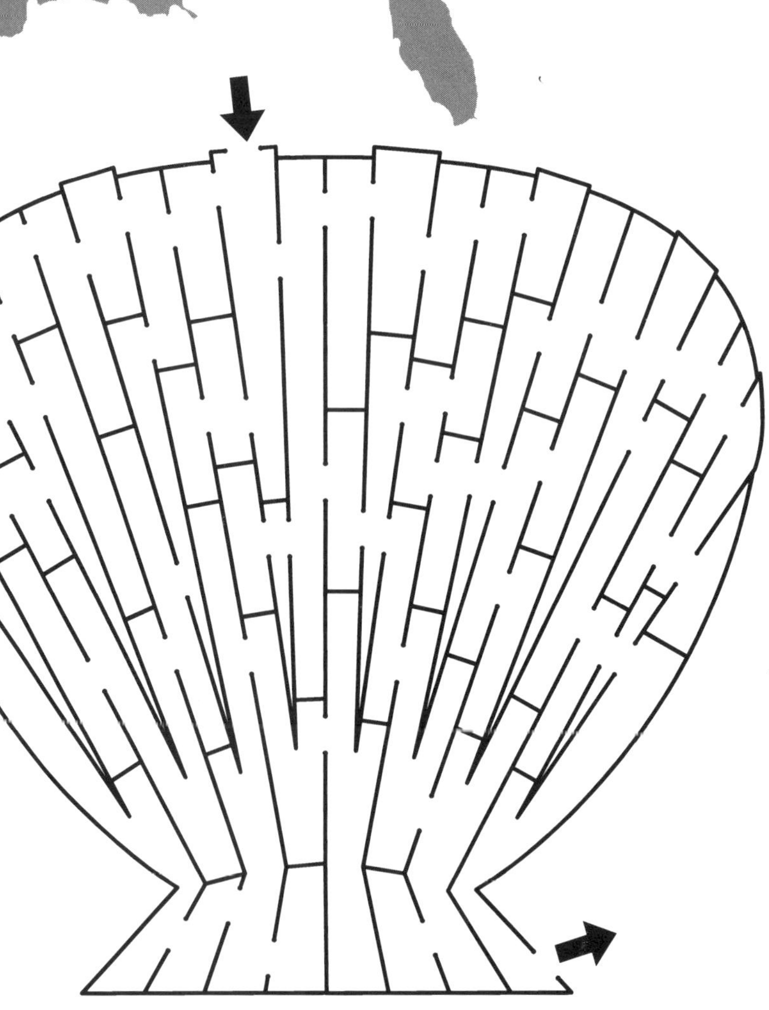

CITY SEARCH

I	T	D	H	I	C	Y	O	P	C	U	K	C	M	I
T	Q	X	N	H	G	E	W	A	R	G	G	U	I	K
Z	J	R	G	K	W	G	E	W	A	Z	L	M	B	D
Y	E	N	Z	B	O	N	C	T	N	X	Y	B	V	C
X	T	W	T	F	O	A	O	U	S	H	A	E	J	J
A	B	T	K	F	N	R	A	C	T	U	F	R	Y	T
H	F	T	B	G	S	R	O	K	O	W	T	L	Q	B
X	X	W	Z	W	O	A	J	E	N	N	O	A	A	S
L	S	E	Y	O	C	G	J	T	Z	E	J	N	V	N
E	D	S	J	C	K	A	T	T	Q	F	N	D	E	S
P	B	T	S	E	E	N	N	M	X	W	O	W	Y	J
V	V	E	M	U	T	S	N	D	U	P	P	D	X	V
G	D	R	Z	T	P	E	Y	F	V	O	O	E	U	Y
U	Q	L	M	X	L	T	Z	B	R	I	S	T	O	L
P	G	Y	N	K	V	T	L	T	Y	Z	H	Q	N	B

BRISTOL
CRANSTON
CUMBERLAND
NARRAGANSETT

NEWPORT
PAWTUCKET
WESTERLY
WOONSOCKET

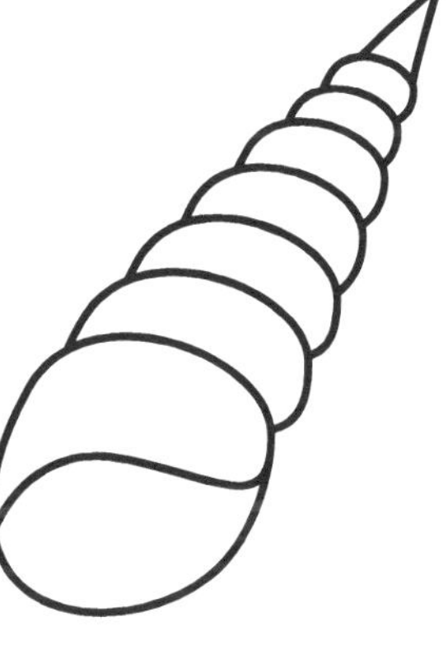

SOUTH CAROLINA

CAPITAL CITY: Columbia
POPULATION: 5,191,000
REGION: Southeastern / South Atlantic
ABBREVIATION: SC
STATE FLOWER: Yellow Jessamine
STATE TREE: Sabal Palm
STATE BIRD: Carolina Wren
STATE NICKNAME: Palmetto State
NATURAL WONDER: Angel Oak

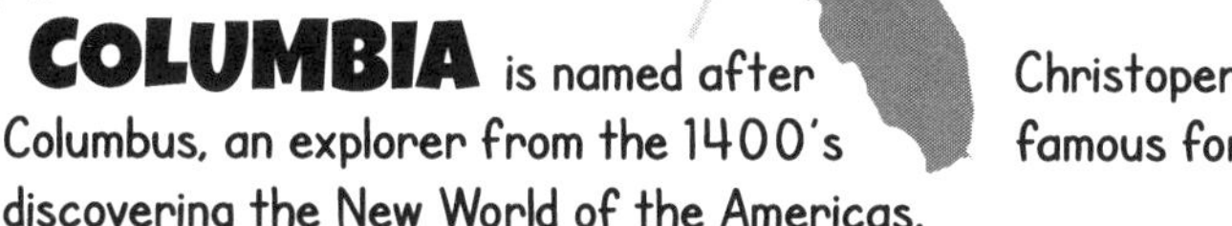

COLUMBIA is named after Christoper Columbus, an explorer from the 1400's famous for discovering the New World of the Americas.

The Carolinas (North and South) were named in honor of King Charles I. In Latin his name is Carolus.

South Carolina's most popular tree, the Sabal Palm or Palmetto, is only one of two palms native to the state. This palm tree is also on the state seal and Mint quarter.

The peach is the official fruit of South Carolina as the state produces the second most in the entire US, behind California. Some call it the peach capital of the world!

The Angel Oak is an old tree with roots tracing back 1,500 years ago.

Sweet tea comes from this state, apparently from the 18th century, as South Carolina was the first state to grow tea plants.

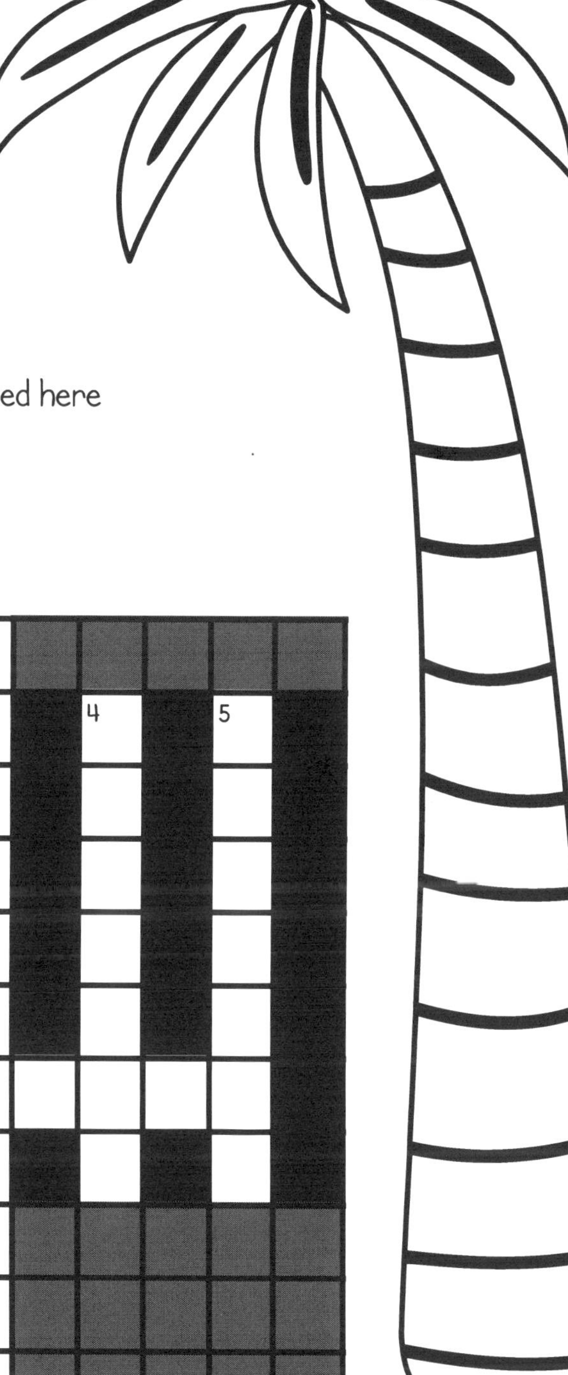

CROSSWORD

Down

2 North neighbor state

3 State tree

4 South West neighbor state

5 King the state was named after

6 1,500 year old tree

Across

1 State bird

3 Tea that originated here

7 State flower

8 Capital city

9 State fruit

SOUTH DAKOTA

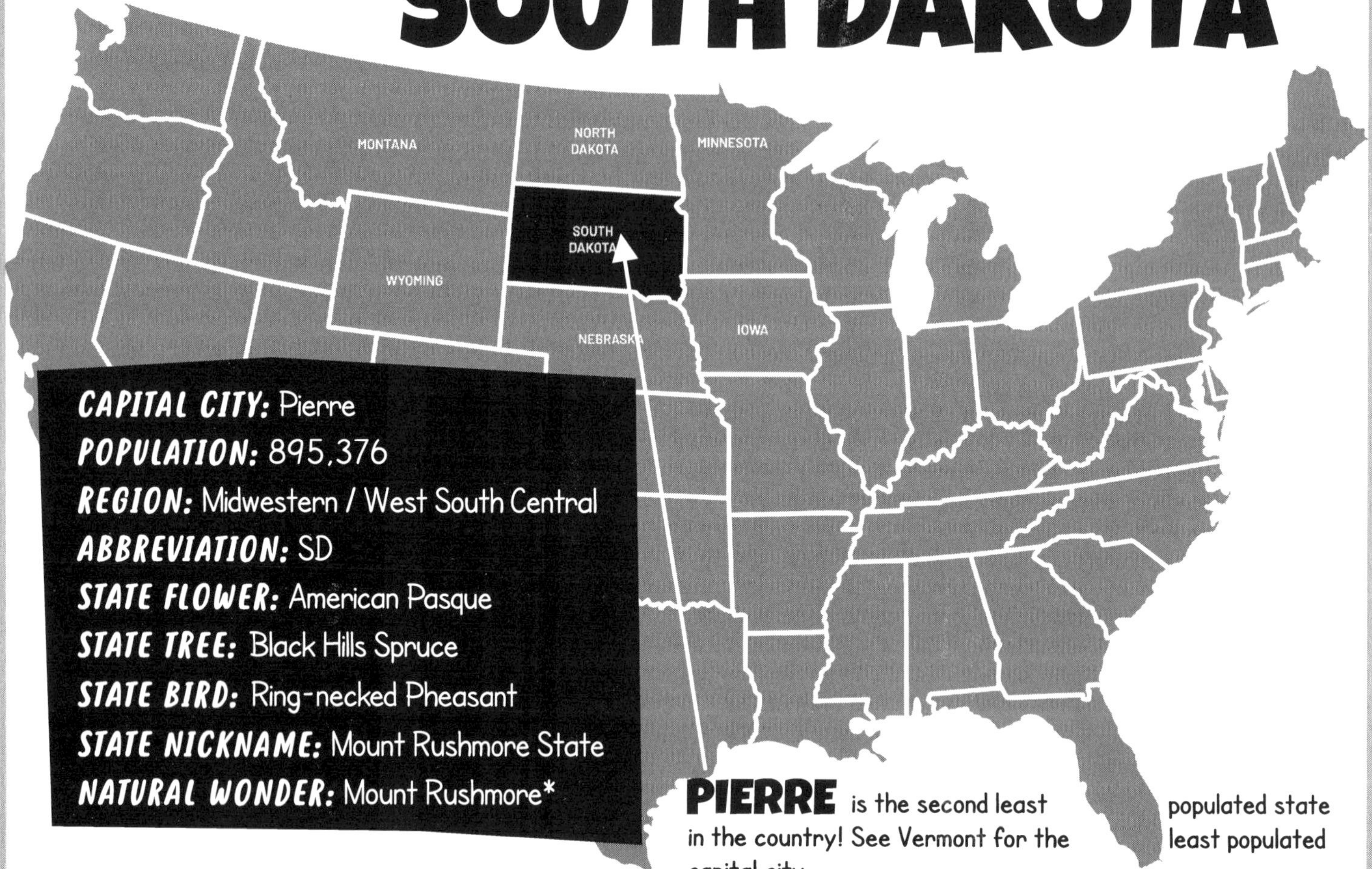

CAPITAL CITY: Pierre
POPULATION: 895,376
REGION: Midwestern / West South Central
ABBREVIATION: SD
STATE FLOWER: American Pasque
STATE TREE: Black Hills Spruce
STATE BIRD: Ring-necked Pheasant
STATE NICKNAME: Mount Rushmore State
NATURAL WONDER: Mount Rushmore*

PIERRE is the second least populated state in the country! See Vermont for the least populated capital city.

This state's nickname comes from a massive sculpture carved into Mount Rushmore of presidents' George Washington, Abraham Lincoln, Thomas Jefferson and Theodore Roosevelt. Also at Black Hills is the Crazy Horse Memorial (under construction since 1948), which will be the second tallest statue in the world when it's finished!

South Dakota has one of the largest America Indian populations, including the Dakota, Lakota and Nakota tribes which form the Sioux Nation.

*technically not a "Natural" wonder as they have been hand carved, but still the most significant landmark in the state.

WORD SCRAMBLE

TUNOM HMRRSUEO	_ _ _ _ _ _ _ _ _ _ _ _ _
RMCNAEAI UPQEAS	_ _ _ _ _ _ _ _ _ _ _ _ _ _
NPAHATES	_ _ _ _ _ _ _ _
EGREGO TNIAHSNGOW	_ _ _ _ _ _ _ _ _ _ _ _ _ _ _ _
HAMRAAB OLCNLNI	_ _ _ _ _ _ _ _ _ _ _ _ _ _
OATSHM NRJEFEOSF	_ _ _ _ _ _ _ _ _ _ _ _ _ _ _
HOEORDTE TROVOLESE	_ _ _ _ _ _ _ _ _ _ _ _ _ _ _ _ _
IPERER	_ _ _ _ _ _
RCYAZ SEHOR	_ _ _ _ _ _ _ _ _ _
OSUIX OTNINA	_ _ _ _ _ _ _ _ _ _ _

DESIGN A QUARTER

What picture can you draw for the state quarter motto "E Pluribus Unum"?

Translated this means "Out of many, one." (Which means out of the many states we are one.)

TENNESSEE

CAPITAL CITY: Nashville
POPULATION: 6,975,000
REGION: Southeastern / East South Central
ABBREVIATION: TN
STATE FLOWER: Iris
STATE TREE: Tulip Poplar
STATE BIRD: Mockingbird
STATE NICKNAME: The Volunteer State
NATURAL WONDER: Tuckaleechee Caverns

Tennessee is a landlocked state known for rock'n'roll and country music. Elvis Presley's home, Graceland, is in Memphis, TN.

NASHVILLE is home to the largest songwriter's festival in the world, Tin Pan South, it is also known as "Music City, USA".

The state has two fault zones, the New Madrid Seismic Zone in the west and the East Tennessee Seismic Zone in the east. This makes earthquakes common in Tennessee.

In the Great Smoky Mountains National Park there are over 30 species of salamander, making it the "Salamander Capital of the World", the most famous being the red salamander. The salamander isn't the state mammal though, the common raccoon is.

WORD MATCHES

TULIP	CAVERN
VOLUNTEER	POPLAR
MUSIC	SALAMANDER
SEISMIC	STATE
RED	SEA
GREAT SMOKY	CITY
COMMON	ZONE
ELVIS	RACCOON
LOST	PRESLEY
UNDERGROUND	MOUNTAINS

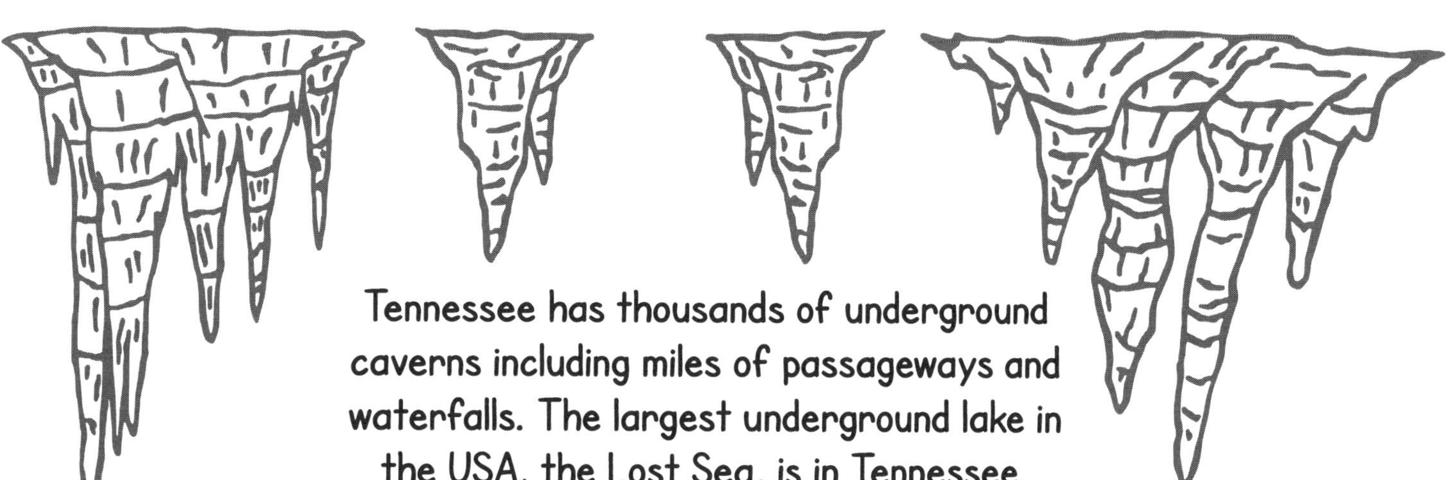

Tennessee has thousands of underground caverns including miles of passageways and waterfalls. The largest underground lake in the USA, the Lost Sea, is in Tennessee.

CRACK THE CODE

Discover the secret caverns in Tennessee

__ 21 __ 8 __ 11 __ 2 __ 5 __ 25 __ 13 __ 13 __ 11 __ 14 __ 13 __ 13

__ 9 __ 8 __ 10 __ 3 __ 5 __ 12

__ 11 __ 8 __ 1 __ 3 __ 13 __ 12 __ 25 __ 5 __ 10 __ 9

KEY

1	2	3	4	5	6	7	8	9	10	11	12	13	14	15	16	17	18	19	20	21	22	23	24	25
M	K	B	O	A	X	Y	U	D	N	C	R	E	H	V	J	W	G	P	Z	T	F	I	Q	L

TEXAS

CAPITAL CITY: Austin
POPULATION: 29,530,000
REGION: West South Central
ABBREVIATION: TX
STATE FLOWER: Bluebonnet
STATE TREE: Pecan Tree
STATE BIRD: Mockingbird
STATE NICKNAME: Lone Star State
NATURAL WONDER: Hamilton Pool

AUSTIN is named after the "Father of Texas", Stephen F. Austin.

Texas is the 2nd largest state in the USA, beaten by Alaska. Due its size it has the most counties in any state, in fact 254!

Austin may be the capital, but Houston, San Antonio and Dallas all have much larger populations.

Should Austin be called Gotham City? It has the largest urban bat colony in the country under Congress Ave Bridge. At the end of bat season more than 1.5 million bats can be seen in the sky.

It is one of four states that border Mexico. Because of this proximity, it has developed a cuisine which is a mix of Mexican and American food called Tex-Mex.

MISSING LETTERS

1. Da_ _a_
2. Te_-_e_
3. S_n An_o_io
4. B_ _s
5. Me_i_o
6. Win_ Fa_ _
7. _ous_on
8. Oi_
9. P_can Tr_ _
10. A_s_in

Texas is famous for its oil, but more recently is known around the world for its wind farms. It has one of the largest wind-power producing farms in the world.

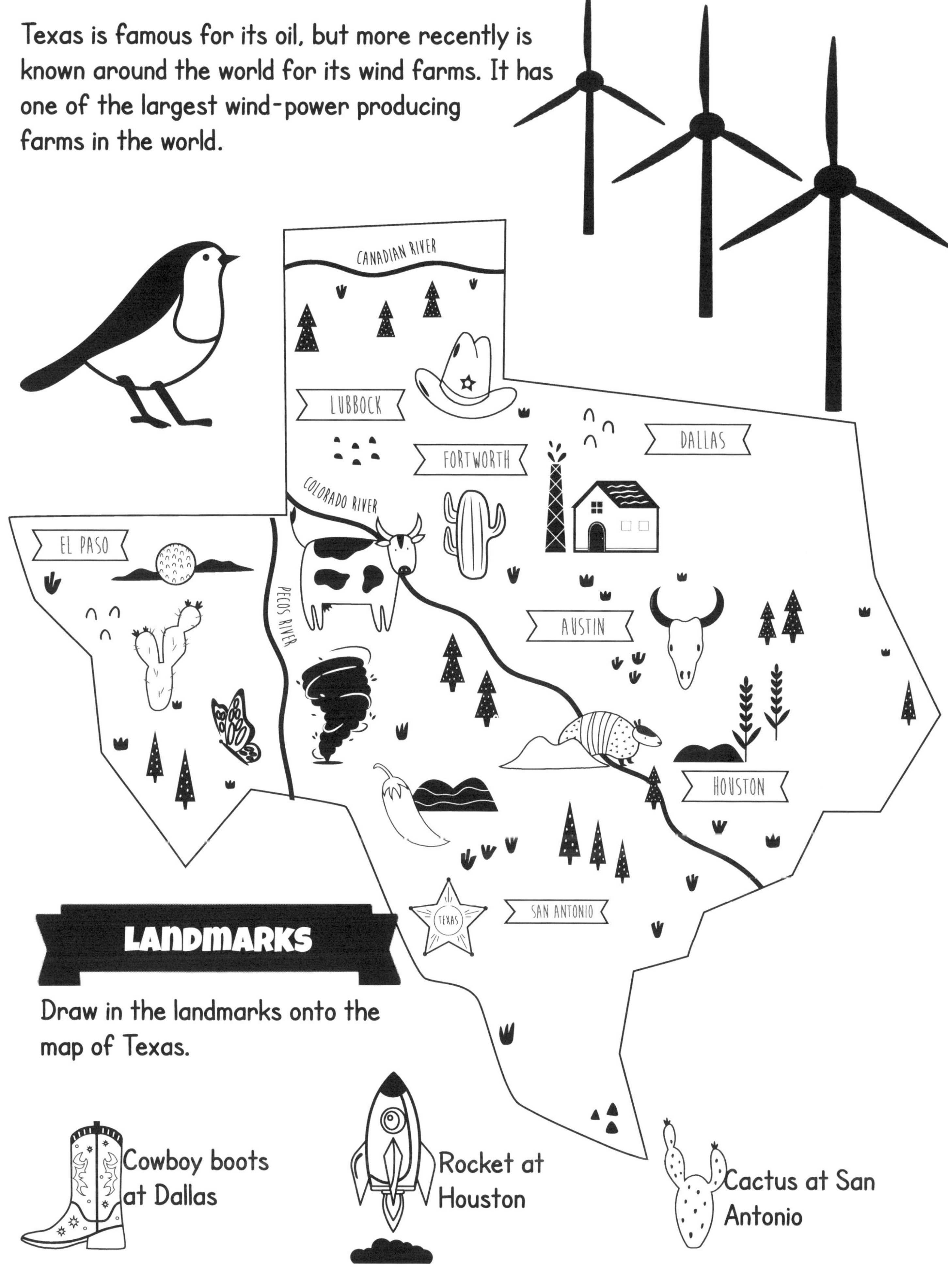

LANDMARKS

Draw in the landmarks onto the map of Texas.

Cowboy boots at Dallas

Rocket at Houston

Cactus at San Antonio

UTAH

CAPITAL CITY: Salt Lake City
POPULATION: 3,338,000
REGION: Western / Mountain States
ABBREVIATION: UT
STATE FLOWER: Sego Lily
STATE TREE: Quaking Aspen
STATE BIRD: Seagull
STATE NICKNAME: The Beehive State
NATURAL WONDER: Arches National Park

SALT LAKE CITY

People believe there are monsters in the Great Salt Lake, they have even named it the North Shore Monster!

Bee AMAZING!

Utah is called The Beehive State because early pioneers thought they were as hardworking as bees!

There is a lot of rock in Utah. Arches National Park has over 2000 natural stone arches and giant balanced rocks. In Monument Valley there are red rock spires, Zion Canyon and Bryce Canyon have rock pillars that look like man-made statues. Between these canyons lies the Grand Staircase, a look into the history of earth with sedimentary rock layers.

Lake Search

V	E	L	S	F	I	L	O	K	O	J	O	O	W	W
T	B	W	V	U	M	V	J	L	J	Z	I	X	E	W
P	M	E	O	I	E	C	A	N	B	T	M	U	R	J
G	N	F	O	G	U	X	V	L	H	U	S	Q	O	Y
D	Z	U	T	A	K	V	A	O	V	R	U	S	H	D
Z	Q	V	P	G	P	N	N	A	V	D	H	P	B	P
V	L	L	P	G	C	H	O	P	O	E	P	O	N	V
Q	K	C	V	H	G	P	L	R	E	I	V	E	S	E
D	G	Q	E	X	O	T	P	G	H	O	G	H	A	G
F	P	W	P	W	K	D	E	L	R	V	L	H	L	U
R	Y	E	E	D	P	V	F	R	S	O	U	T	T	H
B	L	L	O	B	J	C	H	R	C	F	R	A	M	X
E	L	Q	G	Q	D	S	Z	M	U	U	X	R	G	A
A	T	T	G	H	I	L	F	U	Y	S	N	C	I	Q
R	N	P	W	F	V	J	P	X	I	R	A	D	F	M

BEAR
BLANCHE
CRET
FISH
MIRROR
NAVAJO
POWELL
RUSH
SALT
SEVIER
UTAK

LAKE

VERMONT

MONTPELIER
is the least populated state capital in the country, but during the daytime the population doubles due to jobs in the city.

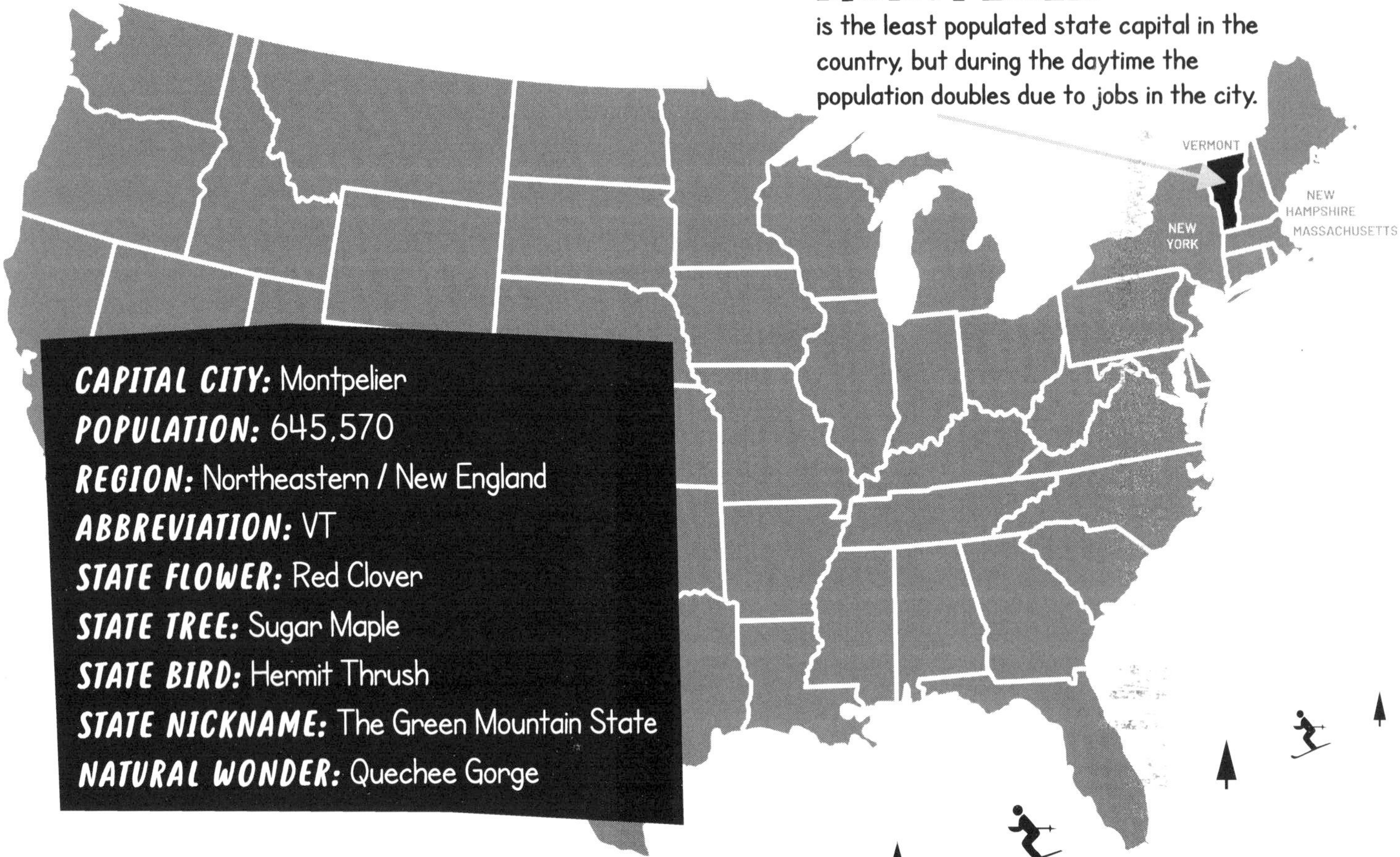

VERMONT
NEW YORK
NEW HAMPSHIRE
MASSACHUSETTS

CAPITAL CITY: Montpelier
POPULATION: 645,570
REGION: Northeastern / New England
ABBREVIATION: VT
STATE FLOWER: Red Clover
STATE TREE: Sugar Maple
STATE BIRD: Hermit Thrush
STATE NICKNAME: The Green Mountain State
NATURAL WONDER: Quechee Gorge

Vermont's nickname comes from two French words, vert mont, which translates to green mountain. Bordering on Canada to the North, to the french speaking province of Quebec, you can easily see the French influence in the region.

The Green Mountains are thought to be some of the oldest rocks in the world, at over 400 million years old.

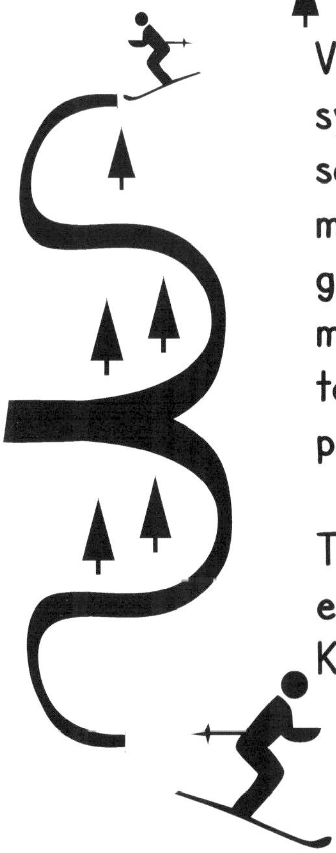

Vermont is famous for maple syrup and it comes from the sap of the state tree. It makes nearly two million gallons a year! This mountainous state has a lot of tall trees like yellow birch, pine, spruce and cedar.

This state is also known for excellent skiing particularly in Killington and Stowe.

CROSSWORD

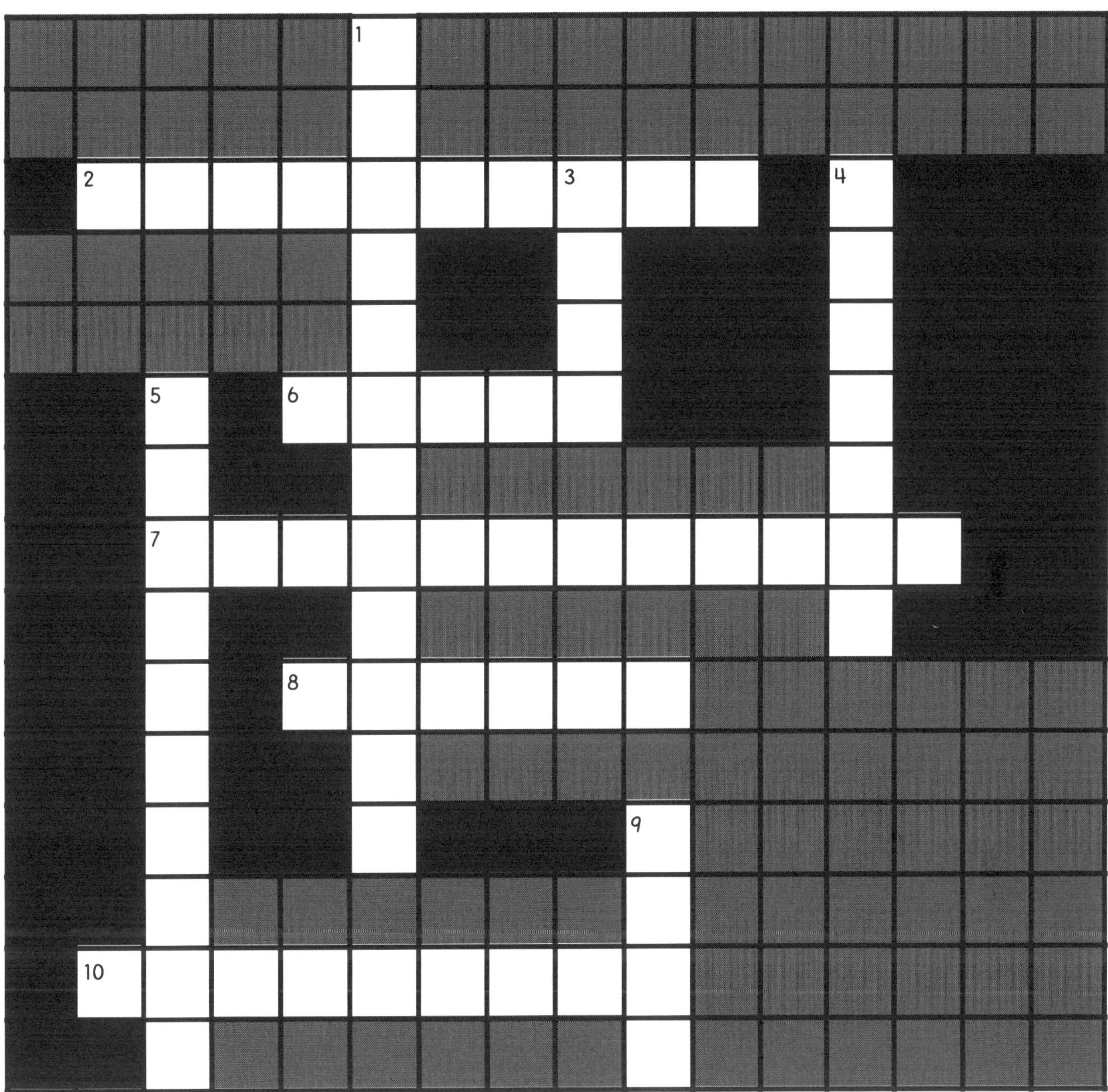

Across

2 State tree

6 Skiing area

7 East neighbor state

8 French speaking neighbor

10 State flower

Down

1 State bird

3 Tall tree

4 West neighbor state

5 Capital city

9 Green in french

VIRGINIA

CAPITAL CITY: Richmond
POPULATION: 8,642,000
REGION: East Coast / South Atlantic
ABBREVIATION: VA
STATE FLOWER & TREE: Dogwood
STATE BIRD: Northern Cardinal
STATE NICKNAME: Old Dominion
NATURAL WONDER: Luray Caverns

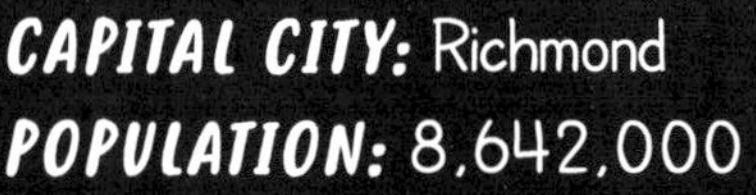

RICHMOND was the Confederacy's capital during the Civil War.

More US presidents were born in Virginia than any other state.

The Pentagon is in Arlington, Virginia and is the world's largest office building. It is home to the Department of Defense.

Virginia was home to the first English colony and was thought of as one of England's dominions. That is where the nickname, Old Dominion State, comes from.

CRACK THE CODE

Which first presidents were born in Virginia?

_ _ _ _ _ _   _ _ _ _ _ _ _ _ _
13 21 12 11 24 2   6 15 4 4 15 1 2 12 14

_ _ _ _ _ _   _ _ _ _ _ _ _ _ _ _
19 15 12 1 19 15   9 24 2 21 8 14 19 13 12 14

KEY

1	2	3	4	5	6	7	8	9	10	11	12	13	14	15	16	17	18	19	20	21	22	23	24	25
R	S	U	F	Q	J	X	I	W	B	M	O	T	N	E	V	P	D	G	L	H	K	C	A	Y

WORD SCRAMBLE

ENGTAONP _ _ _ _ _ _ _ _ _

GNLRNTIAO _ _ _ _ _ _ _ _ _ _

EENRSPIDST _ _ _ _ _ _ _ _ _ _ _

MHNCDOIR _ _ _ _ _ _ _ _

OOODDGW _ _ _ _ _ _ _

DOL OIIDNNOM ASTET _ _ _   _ _ _ _ _ _ _ _   _ _ _ _ _

NACDRLIA _ _ _ _ _ _ _ _

AYRLU ANRVECS _ _ _ _ _   _ _ _ _ _ _ _

GSHILEN _ _ _ _ _ _ _

WASHINGTON

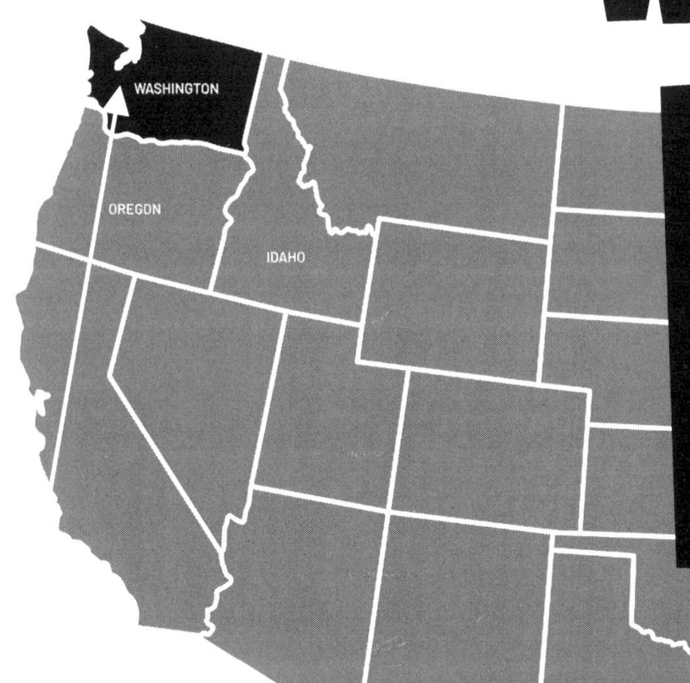

CAPITAL CITY: Olympia
POPULATION: 7,739,000
REGION: Pacific Northwest
ABBREVIATION: WA
STATE FLOWER: Coast Rhododendron
STATE TREE: Western Hemlock
STATE BIRD: American Goldfinch
STATE NICKNAME: The Evergreen State
NATURAL WONDER: Mt Rainier

OLYMPIA
is the capital of Washington State, however you are probably more familiar with Seattle and the Space Needle.

Washington State borders British Columbia in Canada to the north. In the northwest corner of the state is the Olympic National Park, a forest so large (1 million acres) that experts think parts of the park haven't been explored!

With half of the state covered in trees, comes a lot of rain, so much so that Seattle is known as the "Rain City". Mt Rainier is not named after the rain, it was named after Rear Admiral Peter Rainier in 1792. It is also known by the Northwest Native name of Tahoma.

Common trees in the forests are Sitka Spruce, Douglas Fir, Western Hemlock and Alpine Larches.

The Space Needle is an observation tower, restaurant and a landmark in Seattle. It was built in 1962 and is 605 ft tall. How long do you think it takes an elevator to reach the top?

It's 41 seconds!

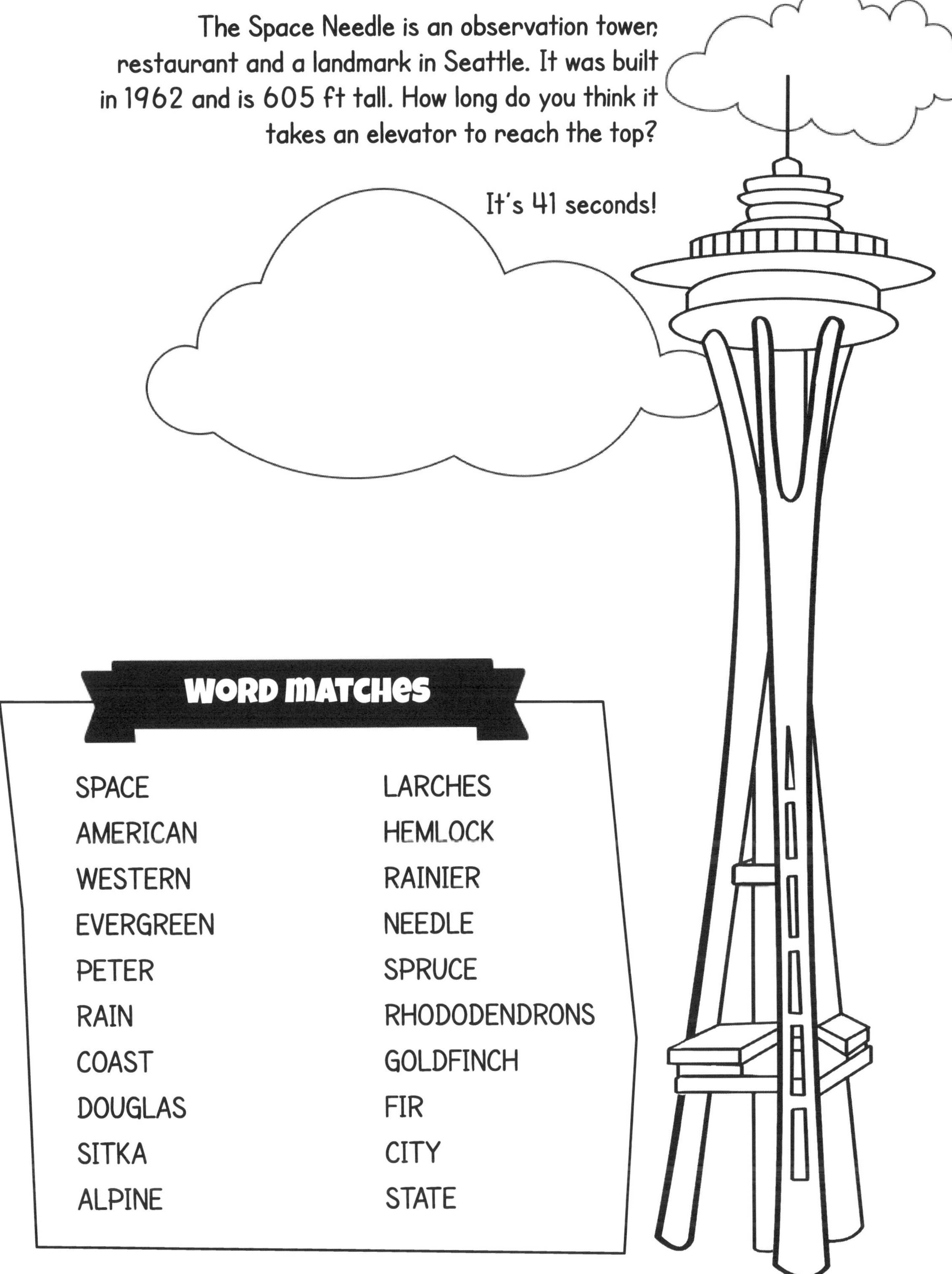

WORD MATCHES

SPACE	LARCHES
AMERICAN	HEMLOCK
WESTERN	RAINIER
EVERGREEN	NEEDLE
PETER	SPRUCE
RAIN	RHODODENDRONS
COAST	GOLDFINCH
DOUGLAS	FIR
SITKA	CITY
ALPINE	STATE

WEST VIRGINIA

CAPITAL CITY: Charleston
POPULATION: 1,783,000
REGION: Southeastern / South Atlantic
ABBREVIATION: WV
STATE FLOWER: Rhododendron
STATE TREE: Sugar Maple
STATE BIRD: Northern Cardinal
STATE NICKNAME: The Mountain State
NATURAL WONDER: Lost World Caverns

PENNSYLVANIA
OHIO
WEST VIRGINIA
MARYLAND
VIRGINIA
KENTUCKY

CHARLESTON is a city of firsts! It has the first public college, the first museum, the first playhouse and the first golf club in the US.

West Virginia is the third most forested state, in fact nearly 80% of the state is covered in forest. The most common trees are hemlock, red spruce, cedar and ash.

New River is not new. In fact this unusual river flows south to north. This uncommon direction was formed before mountains, making it one of the oldest rivers in the world.

The state is also known for its salt. Before it was the first industry to be developed in the state, the local deer and buffalo were licking all the salt they desired at a salt spring on the Kanawha River.

MISSING LETTERS

1. R_o_o_en_ron
2. He_ _ock
3. Ce_a_
4. _har_es_on
5. Ne_ Ri_e_
6. _alt
7. Fo_es_
8. _anaw_a _i_er
9. D_ _r
10. _u_fa_o

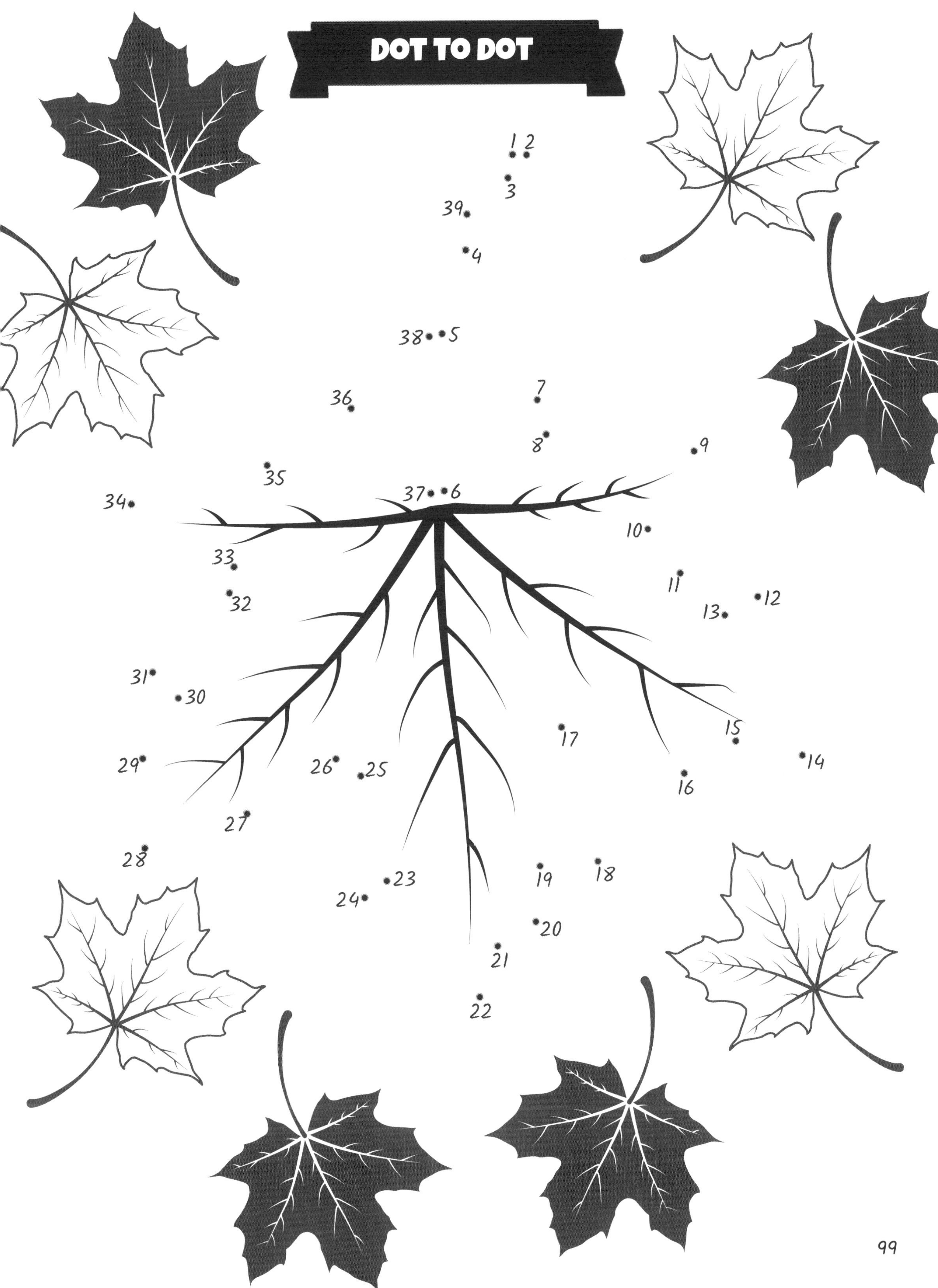
DOT TO DOT
1
2
3
39
4
38
5
36
7
8
9
35
34
37
6
10
33
11
32
12
13
31
30
15
17
29
26
25
14
16
27
28
23
19
18
24
20
21
22

WISCONSIN

MADISON is one of only two major cities built on an isthmus, a narrow strip of land that connects two larger landmasses and separates two bodies of water.

CAPITAL CITY: Madison
POPULATION: 5,896,000
REGION: Midwest / East North Central
ABBREVIATION: WI
STATE FLOWER: Wood Violet
STATE TREE: Sugar Maple
STATE BIRD: American Robin
STATE NICKNAME: Badger State
NATURAL WONDER: Apostle Islands National Lakeshore

This state is home to 14,500 year old mammoth bones, with markings that look like human made tools, suggesting that people have lived in the area before Native American tribes formed thousands of years later.

Wisconsin also has a lot of lakes, more than the Land of 10,000 Lakes (Minnesota). The state has 15,000 created in the last ice age.

WI is home to Bratwurst, a German sausage. Every Memorial Day it hosts the "World's Largest Brat Fest". It sounds like a festival of naughty children, but it's actually a festival of sausage and hot dogs, music, live events and fireworks.

CITY SEARCH

K	J	H	K	K	E	K	S	P	X	Z	C	X	L	D
Z	X	W	D	M	I	L	W	A	U	K	E	E	B	N
V	Q	V	V	D	J	A	M	R	Z	P	S	W	F	Z
I	O	F	J	A	N	E	S	V	I	L	L	E	A	F
K	P	E	D	T	I	P	J	O	S	H	K	O	S	H
J	Z	N	S	B	H	R	M	E	P	X	J	G	T	J
N	W	W	A	U	K	E	S	H	A	N	Z	A	Q	N
O	N	T	J	N	O	S	I	D	A	M	C	W	A	J
T	K	D	I	Q	A	N	N	O	J	L	Y	G	I	T
E	W	A	U	W	A	T	O	S	A	C	Y	G	X	S
L	N	O	A	W	C	W	T	N	J	O	V	E	P	W
P	A	K	E	N	O	S	H	A	B	R	D	N	P	I
P	Q	K	W	Y	R	P	K	E	S	O	H	O	T	Q
A	T	Q	L	T	T	E	H	Y	Q	W	V	W	Q	B
T	Q	W	M	U	X	S	G	C	R	K	O	S	L	H

APPLETON
JANESVILLE
KENOSHA
MADISON
MILWAUKEE
OSHKOSH
SHEBOYGAN
WAUKESHA
WAUWATOSA

WYOMING

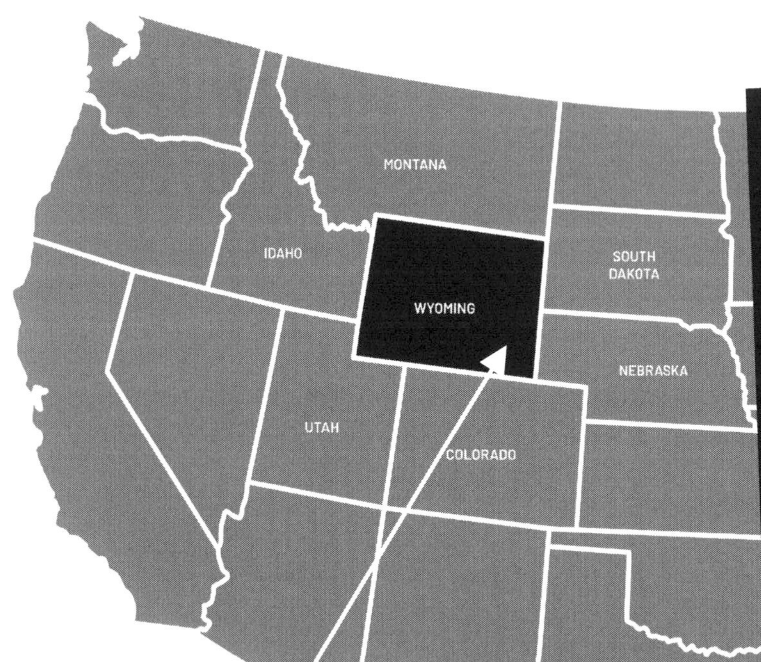

CAPITAL CITY: Cheyenne
POPULATION: 578,803
REGION: Western / Mountain States
ABBREVIATION: WY
STATE FLOWER: Indian Paintbrush
STATE TREE: Plains Cottonwood
STATE BIRD: Western Meadowlark
STATE NICKNAME: The Equality State
NATURAL WONDER: Yellowstone National Park

CHEYENNE

is named by squatters for the Cheyenne Indians which were removed from the land in 1867 by the Union Pacific Railroad.

Wyoming is called the Equality State as it was the first state to grant women the right to vote.

Yellowstone National Park is the world's first national park and is home to about half of the world's active geysers. A famous geyser in the park erupts almost every one and half hours, so predictable that it is named Old Faithful.

The park is also home to the fictitious Yogi Bear, and there are lots of black bears in the park, as well as grizzlies. In fact the park has loads of animals with 300 species of birds and 67 different mammals.

CROSSWORD

Across

4 World's 1st national park

8 State tree

9 Type of bears in Yellowstone

10 South west neighbor

Down

1 North neighbor state

2 Hot spring that erupts

3 Famous geyser that erupts regularly

5 State's nickname

6 Second half of state bird's name

7 Famous bear

ANSWERS

ALABAMA WORD SCRABBLE

Page 4

CTEKOR	=	ROCKET
TFALOOLB	=	FOOTBALL
RONI	=	IRON
ELETS	=	STEEL
TTNOCO	=	COTTON
ASAN	=	NASA
LIIVC	=	CIVIL
EALCRBBYKR	=	BLACKBERRY
EDIIX	=	DIXIE

ALABAMA MAP

Page 5

ALASKA WORD SEARCH

Page 7

ALASKA MAP

Page 6

ARIZONA WORD SEARCH

Page 8

FOUR	TOWN
SAGUARO	BRIDGE
GHOST	DATE
METEOR	CACTUS
COPPER	BREAD
LONDON	CORNERS
FRY	CRATE
MEDJOOL	MINING

ARIZONA MAZE

Page 9

ARKANSAS MISSING LETTERS

Page 10

1. Little Rock
2. Pink Tomato
3. Mockingbird
4. Apple Blossom
5. Rice
6. Natural State
7. Caverns
8. Mountain
9. River
10. Forest

CALIFORNIA MAP

Page 13

CALIFORNIA WORD SEARCH

Page 12

COLORADO WORD SCRABBLE

Page 14

GNIISK	=	SKIING
DRE	=	RED
SNIHPSA	=	SPANISH
OEDWRLIFLWS	=	WILDFLOWERS
OAROOLDC	=	COLORADO
NUITNOASM	=	MOUNTAINS
RUNATE	=	NATURE
SEIRRV	=	RIVERS
PNGMICA	=	CAMPING

COLORADO MAZE

Page 15

CONNECTICUT WORD MATCHES

Page 16

MOUNTAIN	ISLAND
AMERICAN	FINN
NEW	ENGLAND
MARK	BEAUTY
CHARTER	HILL
ROCKY	STATE
COASTAL	OAK
LONG	ROBIN
HUCKLEBERRY	TWAIN
NUTMEG	LAUREL

COLORADO SOLVE THE SEQUENCE

Page 15

DELAWARE MISSING LETTERS

Page 18

1. Blue Hen
2. Mid Atlantic
3. First State
4. New Castle
5. Blackbird
6. Swampland
7. Kent
8. Peach Blossom
9. Sussex
10. Redden

DELAWARE CRACK THE CODE

Page 19

ATLANTIC

COASTAL

PLAIN

FLORIDA WORD SEARCH

Page 21

												E		
		R		I	M	A	I	M			N			
			E							I				A
				T					H		K			L
	M				I			S		E				L
		I				R	N		Y				E	I
			A			U	E	S				V		G
				M	S		B	M			E			A
					I	E		O	E	R				T
					A		R		G	N				O
				C		A		L			T		E	R
			H		N		A					C		S
		E		G		D					A			
	S		E		E					P				
		S		S					S					

FLORIDA MAP

Page 20

PENSACOLA

Orlando

DAYTONA BEACH

DISNEYLAND

Cape Canaveral

Lake Okeechobee

WEST PALM BEACH

MIAMI

GEORGIA CROSSWORD

Page 23

			1 P																
			E																
2 I	S	L	A	N	D	3 S		4 O											
			C			P		K								10 L			
			H			R		E								I			
						I		F								V			
						N		E			5 Y					E			
			6 K	I	N	G		N			A					O			
						7 S	T	O	N	E	M	O	U	N	T	A	I	N	
								K			A					K			
								E			C								
								E			R			8 R					
											9 A	T	L	A	N	T	A		
											W								

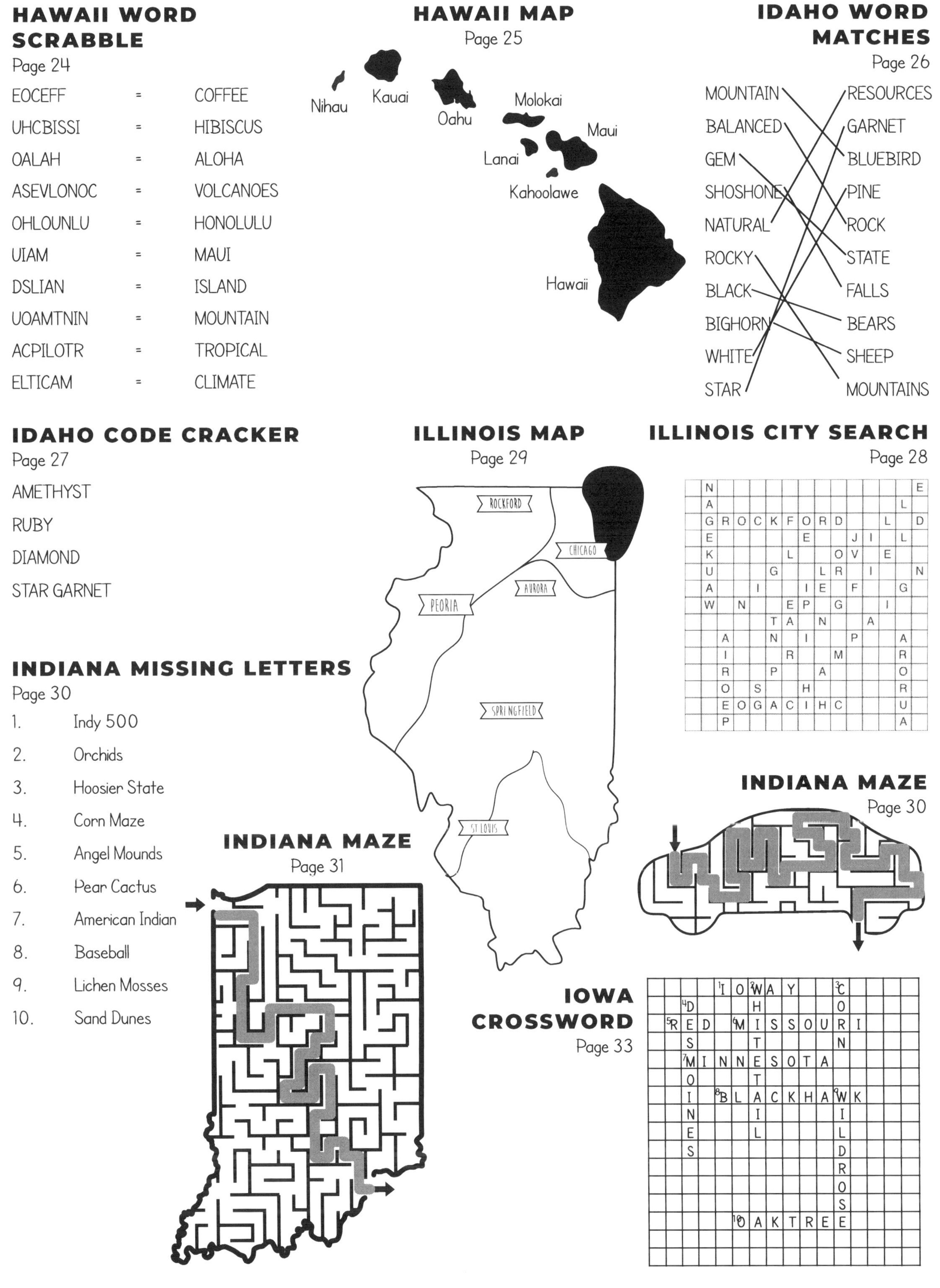

HAWAII WORD SCRABBLE
Page 24
EOCEFF = COFFEE
UHCBISSI = HIBISCUS
OALAH = ALOHA
ASEVLONOC = VOLCANOES
OHLOUNLU = HONOLULU
UIAM = MAUI
DSLIAN = ISLAND
UOAMTNIN = MOUNTAIN
ACPILOTR = TROPICAL
ELTICAM = CLIMATE
HAWAII MAP
Page 25
Nihau
Kauai
Oahu
Molokai
Maui
Lanai
Kahoolawe
Hawaii
IDAHO WORD MATCHES
Page 26
MOUNTAIN
BALANCED
GEM
SHOSHONE
NATURAL
ROCKY
BLACK
BIGHORN
WHITE
STAR
RESOURCES
GARNET
BLUEBIRD
PINE
ROCK
STATE
FALLS
BEARS
SHEEP
MOUNTAINS
IDAHO CODE CRACKER
Page 27
AMETHYST
RUBY
DIAMOND
STAR GARNET
ILLINOIS MAP
Page 29
ROCKFORD
CHICAGO
AURORA
PEORIA
SPRINGFIELD
ST LOUIS
ILLINOIS CITY SEARCH
Page 28
INDIANA MISSING LETTERS
Page 30
1. Indy 500
2. Orchids
3. Hoosier State
4. Corn Maze
5. Angel Mounds
6. Pear Cactus
7. American Indian
8. Baseball
9. Lichen Mosses
10. Sand Dunes
INDIANA MAZE
Page 30
INDIANA MAZE
Page 31
IOWA CROSSWORD
Page 33
IOWAY
WHITETAIL
CORN
DES MOINES
RED
MISSOURI
MINNESOTA
BLACKHAWK
WILD ROSES
OAK TREE

KANSAS WORD SCRABBLE

Page 35

OPAKET	=	TOPEKA
EWLFROUSN	=	SUNFLOWER
IMDTSEW	=	MIDWEST
ATSLLSGRA	=	TALLGRASS
IIHACTW	=	WICHITA
OTANODR	=	TORNADO
ZWAIDR	=	WIZARD
ATLS	=	SALT
NIME	=	MINE
NODWOOTCOT	=	COTTONWOOD

KENTUCKY WORD SCRABBLE

Page 36

KENTUCKY	VALLEY
TULIP	COUNTY
NORTHERN	CAVE
BLUEGRASS	DERBY
JEFFERSON	PEARL
ABRAHAM	KNOX
FORT	POPLAR
MAMMOTH	LINCOLN
FRESHWATER	STATE
RIVER	CARDINAL

KENTUCKY MAZE

Page 37

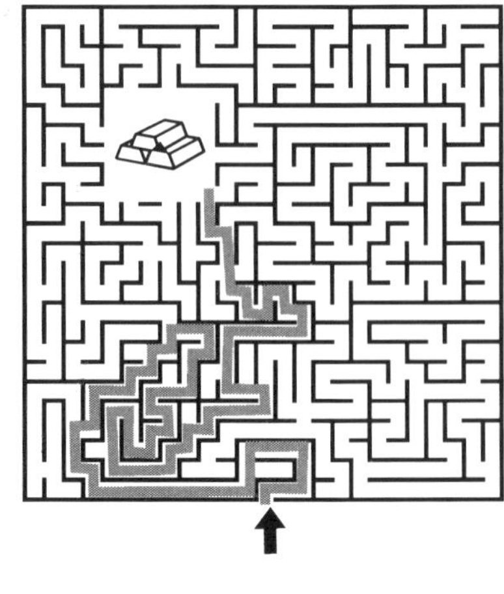

KANSAS MAP

Page 35

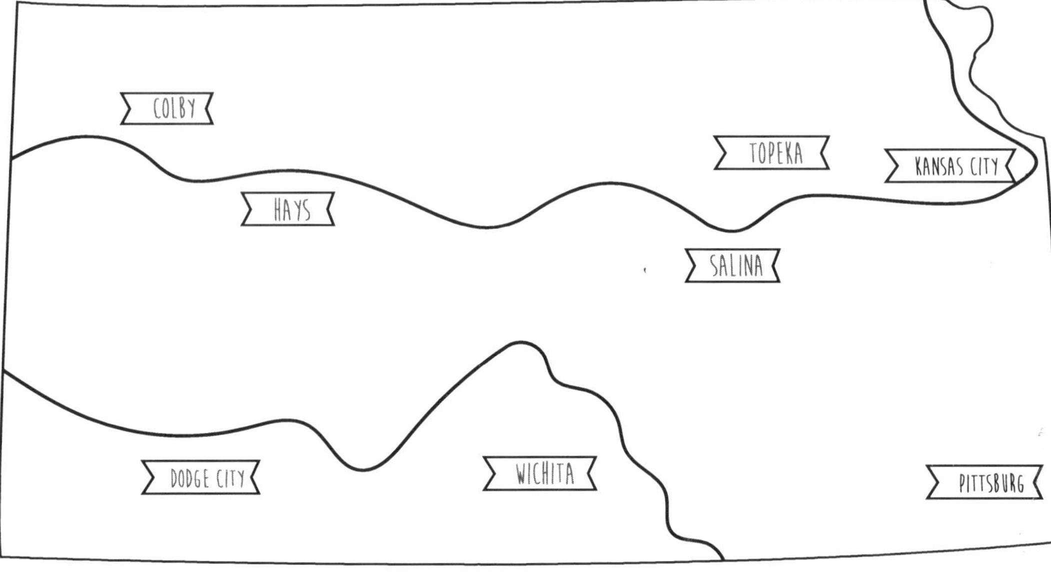

LOUISIANA MISSING LETTERS

Page 38

1. BATON ROUGE
2. CREOLE
3. PELICAN STATE
4. SEVEN SISTERS
5. CAJUN
6. BROWN PELICAN
7. MISSISSIPPI RIVER
8. NEW ORLEANS
9. JAZZ
10. BALD CYPRESS

MAINE EYE SPY

Page 40

MAINE WORD SEARCH

Page 41

MARYLAND CROSSWORD

Page 43

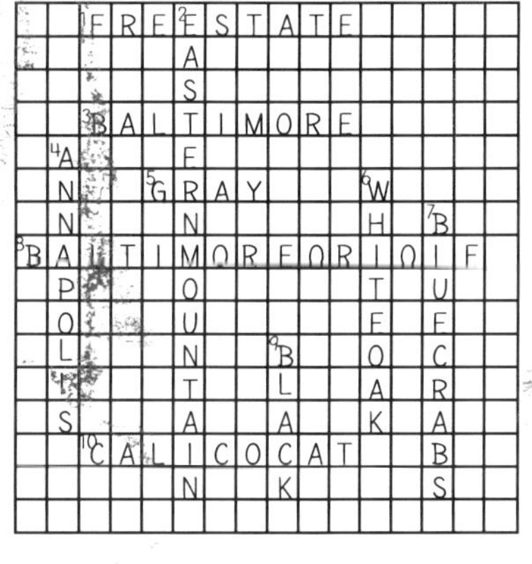

MASSACHUSETTS WORD SCRABBLE

Page 44

YFMRLWAOE	=	MAYFLOWER
DCAKHIECE	=	CHICKADEE
SNBOOT	=	BOSTON
IIHGNTGASKNV	=	THANKSGIVING
MULPOYTH	=	PLYMOUTH
RTA	=	ART
RBAENYRRC	=	CRANBERRY
IEGLHUTOHS	=	LIGHTHOUSE
LIMPIRG	=	PILGRIM

MICHIGAN WORD MATCHES

Page 46

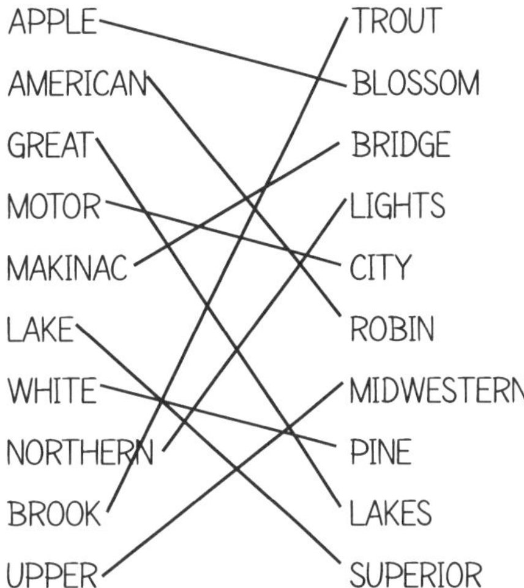

MINNESOTA MISSING LETTERS

Page 48

1. Red Pine
2. Niagara Cave
3. Stalagmite
4. North Star State
5. Limestone
6. Fossil
7. Stalactites
8. Raccoon
9. Bobcat
10. Muskrat

MINNESOTA CRACK THE CODE

Page 49

Rainy Lake

Lake Superior

Lake Minnetonka

MINNESOTA RACCOON MAZE

Page 49

MISSOURI WORD SEARCH

Page 53

					N	O	S	N	A	R	B			
			S	P	R	I	N	G	F	I	E	L	D	
	I			N										
	N			O		N	K							
A	D			S		Q	R	A						
I	E			R	B	B		O	N					
B	P			E	L	B			H	S				
M	E			F	U					T	A			
U	N			F	E			O			W	S		
L	D			E	B			Z				A		
O	E			J	I			A					H	
C	N				R			R						
	C				D			K						
	E							S						

MISSISSIPPI CROSSWORD

Page 51

1 JACKSON (across)
1 JACKSON STATE UNIVERSITY (down)
2 COTTON
3 MOCKINGBIRD
4 ELVIS PRESLEY
5 OPRAHWINFREY
6 MAGNOLIA
7 UNIVERSITYOFMISSISSIPPI
8 PETRIFIEDFOREST
9 MISSIPPI

MONTANA WORD SCRAMBLE

Page 54

LGOD	=	GOLD
TOBRRTEOII	=	BITTERROOT
NAELEH	=	HELENA
INSAMOUNT	=	MOUNTAINS
LERIVS	=	SILVER
SRRAUETE	=	TREASURE
LEIRNMSIOALI	=	MILLIONAIRES
ARBES	=	BEARS
SBOIN	=	BISON
EWVSOL	=	WOLVES

MONTANA MAZE

Page 55

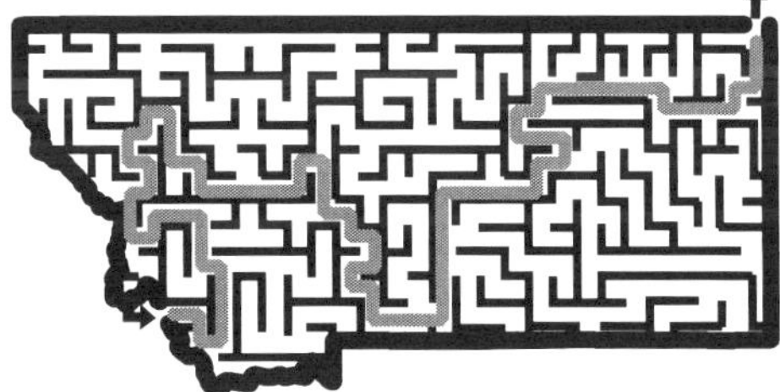

NEBRASKA WORD MATCHES

Page 56

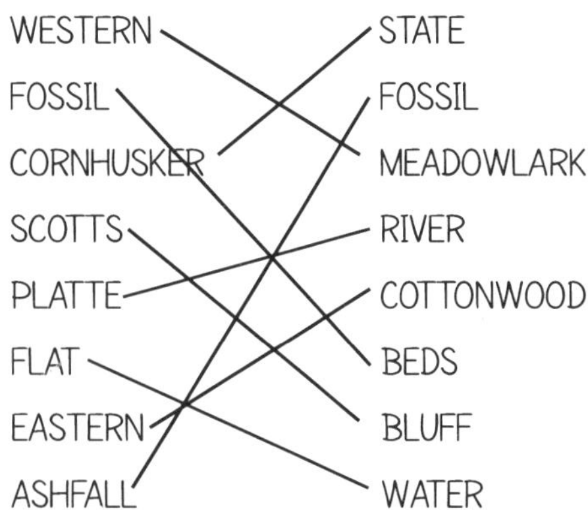

WESTERN	STATE
FOSSIL	FOSSIL
CORNHUSKER	MEADOWLARK
SCOTTS	RIVER
PLATTE	COTTONWOOD
FLAT	BEDS
EASTERN	BLUFF
ASHFALL	WATER

NEVADA MISSING LETTERS

Page 58

1. Las Vegas
2. Silver State
3. Mayflower
4. Sagebrush
5. Kit Carson
6. Sierra Nevada
7. Rattlesnake
8. Tortoise
9. Valley of Fire
10. Wild Horses

NEW HAMPSHIRE CITY SEARCH

Page 61

			L	O	N	D	O	N	D	E	R	R	Y	M
	Y	K											A	
S		R	C									N		
A	R		R	A	H	U	D	S	O	N	C			
L		E		E	M					H				
E			V		D	I			E					
M				O			R	S						
					D		T	R						
						E			E					
					R					M				
		N	A	S	H	U	A							
							C	O	N	C	O	R	D	
					R	O	C	H	E	S	T	E	R	

NEBRASKA CRACK THE CODE

Page 57

RACCOON DOGS

SABER-TOOTH DEER

GIRAFFE CAMELS

NEW JERSEY CROSSWORD

Page 63

1 G													2 V		
A				3 S	T	E	R	L	I	N	G	H	I	L	L
R				Q									O		
D				U			6 M	O	7 N	O	P	O	L	Y	
E		4 T		A					J				E		
N		R		R			5 B						T		
S		E		E			O								
T		N					A								
A		T					R								
8 T	H	O	M	A	S	E	D	I	S	O	N				
E		N					W								
							A								
					9 G	O	L	D	F	I	N	C	H		
							K								
							S								

NEW MEXICO MAZE

Page 65

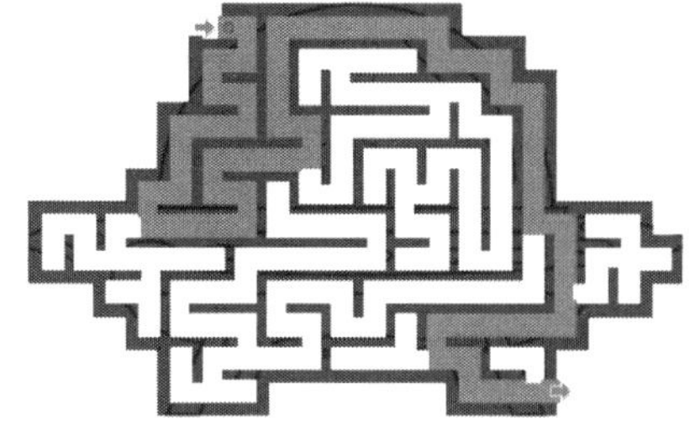

NEW YORK TAXIS

Page 67

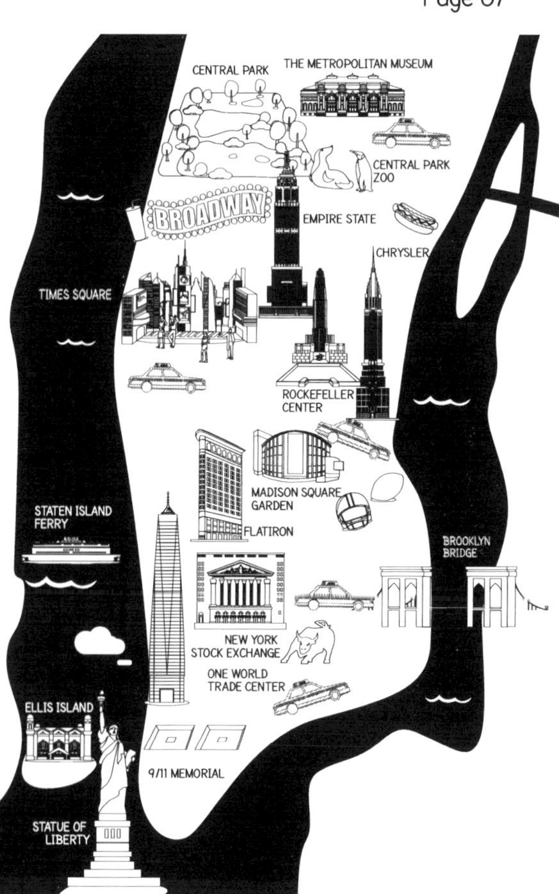

NEW YORK WORD MATCHES

Page 66

NIAGARA	STATION
EMPIRE	FALLS
SUGAR	BLUEBIRD
ELLIS	MAPLE
CENTRAL	AMSTERDAM
FINGER	STATE
ERIE	ISLAND
EASTERN	LAKES
NEW	CANAL
RAILWAY	PARK

NEW MEXICO WORD SCRAMBLE

Page 64

YNSNU	=	SUNNY
ACYUC	=	YUCCA
PUYGMS	=	GYPSUM
NSDA	=	SAND
OMITNUNA	-	MOUNTAIN
LSRSDAANG	=	GRASSLAND
SIANLE	=	ALIENS
EWLLRSO	=	ROSWELL
RETDSE	=	DESERT
EODNRRURNA	=	ROADRUNNER

NORTH CAROLINA MISSING LETTERS

Page 68

1. Kitty Hawk
2. Dogwood
3. Jockey's Ridge
4. Tar Heel State
5. Furniture
6. Oak Trees
7. Coastal Plain
8. Outer Banks
9. Barrier Islands
10. Mainland

NORTH DAKOTA WORD SEARCH

Page 71

					T		H		F			S		
					U		O		I			C		
					R		N	B	S			A		
		B			T	O	E	U	H			N		
			I		L	I	Y	F	I			D		
				S	E	L		F	N			I		
O					M			A	G			N		
G					O	A		L				A		S
R					U		R	O				V		R
A					N			K				I		E
F					T							A		V
					A							N		I
					I									R
					N									
					S									

OHIO CORN MA(I)ZE

Page 72

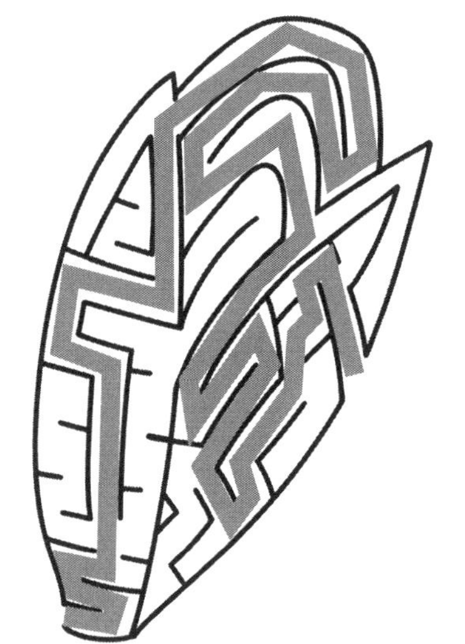

OHIO CROSSWORD

Page 73

					1 I	N	2 D	I	A	N	A		
							A						
3 K	E	N	4 T	U	C	K	Y			5 C		6 C	
			I				T			L		A	
			L				O			E		R	
			L				N			V		D	
			P							E		I	
	7 K	E	L	L	E	Y	S	I	S	L	A	N	D
8 B			A							A		A	
U			I							N		L	
9 C	A	R	N	A	T	I	10 O	N		D			
K			S				H						
E													
Y													
E													

OKLAHOMA WORD SCRAMBLE

Page 74

DUEBRD	=	REDBUD
YLTHCFCRAE	=	FLYCATCHER
RKLBUACE	=	ARBUCKLE
UTSAL	=	TULSA
ILO	=	OIL
RSNOOE TESAT	=	SOONER STATE
SOER	=	ROSE
TLAS LAPNIS	=	SALT PLAINS
IBNSO	=	BISON
AHITCIW	=	WICHITA

OKLAHOMA CRACK THE CODE

Page 75

PONTOTOC

CARTER

JOHNSTON

MURRAY

OREGON WORD MATCHES

Page 76

DOUGLAS	LAKE
OREGON	STATE
WESTERN	PLOVER
BEAVER	PARK
CRATER	FIR
GRAY	FACTORY
SNOWY	OWLS
MILL ENDS	GRAPE
CHEESE	MEADOWLARK
BURROWING	WOLVES

PENNSYLVANIA MISSING LETTERS

Page 79

KEYSTONE STATE

MOUNTAIN LAUREL

BLACK BEARS

PHILADELPHIA

MEADOWCRAFT ROCKSHELTER

PINE CREEK GORGE

RED FOXES

HARRISBURG

RUFFED GROUSE

PENNSYLVANIA

RHODE ISLAND MAZE

Page 80

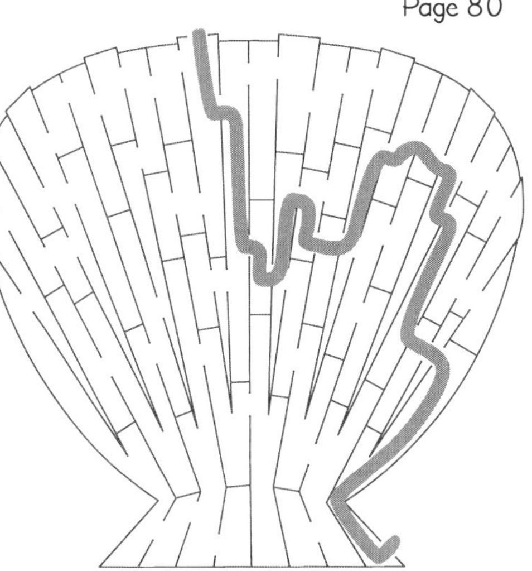

RHODE ISLAND CITY SEARCH
Page 81

								P	C			C		
								A	R			U		
					W			W	A			M		
					O	N		T	N			B		
					O	A		U	S			E		
					N	R		C	T			R		
					S	R		K	O			L		
		W			O	A		E	N			A		
		E			C	G		T				N		N
		S			K	A						D	E	
		T			E	N						W		
		E			T	S					P			
		R				E				O				
		L				T		B	R	I	S	T	O	L
		Y				T		T						

SOUTH CAROLINA MAZE
Page 82

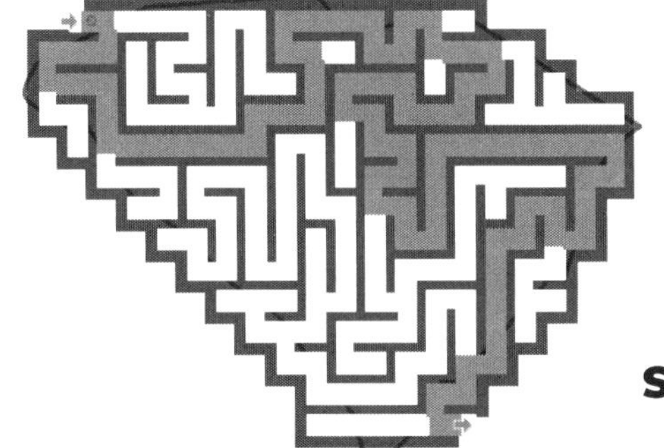

TENNESSEE CRACK THE CODE
Page 87

TUCKALEECHEE

DUNBAR

CUMBERLAND

SOUTH DAKOTA WORD SCRAMBLE
Page 85

TUNOM HMRRSUEO	=	MOUNT RUSHMORE
RMCNAEAI UPQEAS	=	AMERICAN PASQUE
NPAHATES	=	PHEASANT
EGREGO TNIAHSNGOW	=	GEORGE WASHINGTON
HAMRAAB OLCNLNI	=	ABRAHAM LINCOLN
OATSHM NRJEFEOSF	=	THOMAS JEFFERSON
HOEORDTE TROVOLESE	=	THEODORE ROOSEVELT
IPERER	=	PIERRE
RCYAZ SEHOR	=	CRAZY HORSE
OSUIX OTNINA	=	SIOUX NATION

SOUTH CAROLINA CROSSWORD
Page 83

1 C	A	R	O	L	I	N	A	W	R	E	2 N					
											O		4 G		5 C	
			3 S	W	E	E	T				R		E		H	
			A					6 A			T		O		A	
			B					N			H		R		R	
			A					G			C		G		L	
	7 Y	E	L	L	O	W	J	E	S	S	A	M	I	N	E	
			P					L			R		A		S	
			A					O			O					
	8 C	O	L	U	M	B	I	A			L					
			M					K			I					
											N					
									9 P	E	A	C	H			

TENNESSEE WORD MATCHES
Page 86

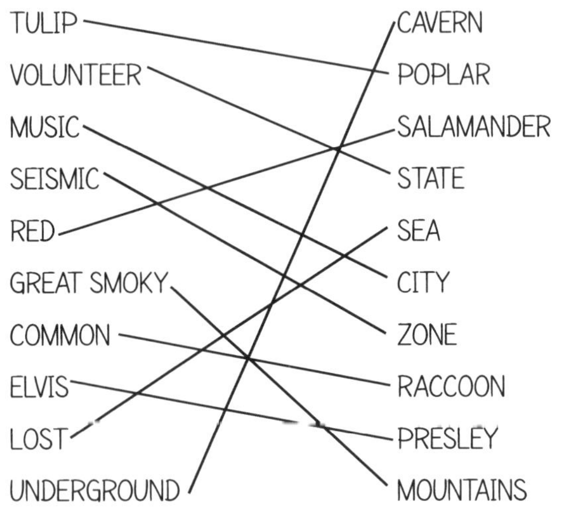

TEXAS MISSING LETTERS
Page 88

1. DALLAS
2. TEX-MEX
3. SAN ANTONIO
4. BATS
5. MEXICO
6. WIND FARM
7. HOUSTON
8. OIL
9. PECAN TREE
10. AUSTIN

TEXAS MAP
Page 89

UTAH BEE A-MAZE-ING

Page 90

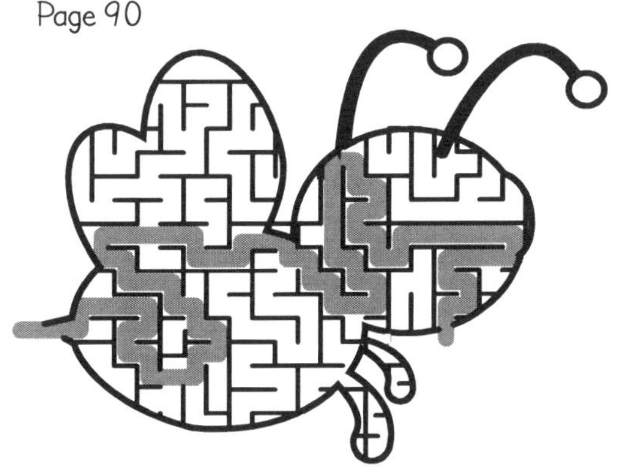

VERMONT CROSSWORD

Page 93

					[1]H										
					E										
	[2]S	U	G	A	R	M	A	[3]P	L	E		[4]N			
					M			I				E			
					I			N				W			
		[5]M		[6]S	T	O	W	E				Y			
		O			T							O			
		[7]N	E	W	H	A	M	P	S	H	I	R	E		
		T			R							K			
		P		[8]Q	U	E	B	E	C						
		E			S										
		L			H				[9]V						
		I							E						
	[10]R	E	D	C	L	O	V	E	R						
		R							T						

VIRGINIA MAZE

Page 94

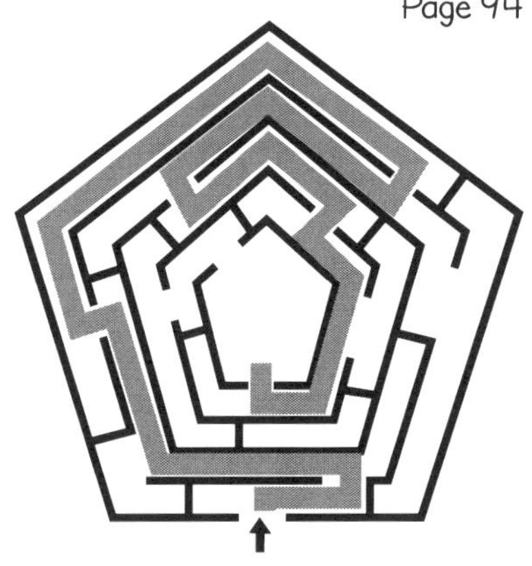

UTAH LAKE SEARCH

Page 91

							O							
							J							
							A		B					
							V	L						
		U	T	A	K		A			R	U	S	H	
						N	N							
					C									
				H		P		R	E	I	V	E	S	
			E		O	T							A	
				W			E		R				L	
			E					R		O			T	
B		L					H		C		R			
E	L					S						R		
A					I								I	
R				F										M

VIRGINIA CRACK THE CODE

Page 95

THOMAS JEFFERSON

GEORGE WASHINGTON

VIRGINIA WORD SCRAMBLE

Page 95

ENGTAONP = PENTAGON

GNLRNTIAO = ARLINGTON

EENRSPIDST = PRESIDENTS

MHNCDOIR = RICHMOND

OOODDGW = DOGWOOD

DOL OIIDNNOM ASTET = OLD DOMINION STATE

NACDRLIA = CARDINAL

AYRLU ANRVECS = LURAY CAVERNS

GSHILEN = ENGLISH

WASHINGTON WORD MATCHES

Page 97

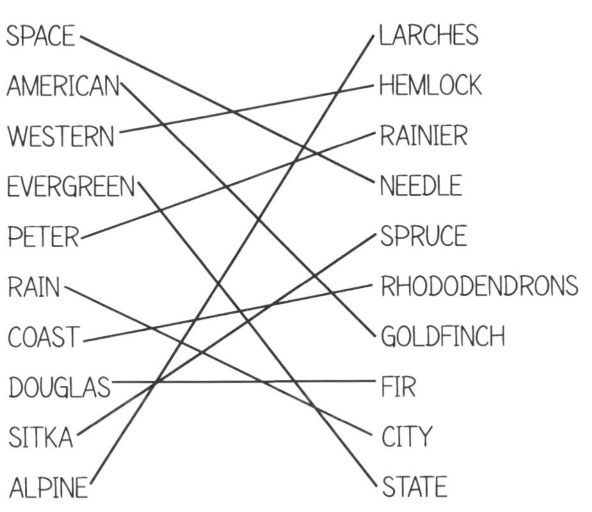

WEST VIRGINIA MISSING LETTERS

Page 98

1. Rhododendron
2. Hemlock
3. Cedar
4. Charleston
5. New River
6. Salt
7. Forest
8. Kanawha River
9. Deer
10. Buffalo

WISCONSIN CITY SEARCH

Page 101

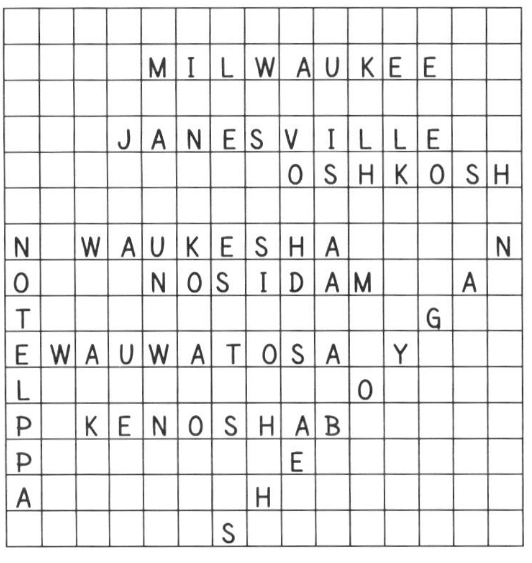

WYOMING MAZE

Page 102

WYOMING CROSSWORD

Page 103

										1M						
										O						
							2G			N						
							E			T						
				3O			Y			A						
	4Y	5E	L	L	O	W	S	T	O	N	E				6M	
		Q		D			E			E					E	
		U		F			R								A	
		A		A				7Y							D	
	8P	L	A	I	N	S	C	O	T	T	O	N	W	O	O	D
		I		T				G							W	
		T		H		9G	R	I	Z	Z	L	Y			L	
		Y		F				B							A	
				U				E							R	
				L		10U	T	A	H						K	
								R								

COUNT THEM UP

The number of times these birds appear:

American Robins: 3

Western Meadowlark: 6

Mockingbirds: 5

The number of times Boris the bear sneaked onto a page: 7

LABEL THE MAP

WASHINGTON
OREGON
CALIFORNIA
IDAHO
NEVADA
MONTANA
WYOMING
UTAH
ARIZONA
COLORADO
NEW MEXICO
NORTH DAKOTA
SOUTH DAKOTA
NEBRASKA
KANSAS
OKLAHOMA
TEXAS
MINNESOTA
IOWA
MISSOURI
ARKANSAS
LOUISIANA
WISCONSIN
ILLINOIS
MICHIGAN
INDIANA
KENTUCKY
TENNESSEE
MISSISSIPPI
ALABAMA
OHIO
WEST VIRGINIA
VIRGINIA
NORTH CAROLINA
SOUTH CAROLINA
GEORGIA
FLORIDA
PENNSYLVANIA
NEW YORK
VERMONT
MAINE
NEW HAMPSHIRE
MASSACHUSETTS
RHODE ISLAND
CONNECTICUT
NEW JERSEY
DELAWARE
MARYLAND
ALASKA
HAWAII

Thank you for purchasing this book!

If you enjoyed this book, please leave us a review on Amazon. It really helps Mrs Huntington continue to produce these workbooks.

See these and the entire range of Mrs Huntington's books at Amazon:

You've finished! Well done! Get a parent to fill in the blanks.

Mrs. Huntington's

Certificate of Achievement

PROUDLY PRESENTED TO

____

For completion of United States Activity Book

______________________ ______________________

Date Signature